CROSS-CURRICULAR TEACHING AND LEARNING IN THE SECONDARY SCHOOL

C000285973

HUMANITIES

What is the role of the humanities in the modern school? Should geography, history, RE and citizenship teachers remain faithful to long-standing subject cultures and pedagogies? Or is there another way to consider how the curriculum, and the notion of individual subjects and teachers' pedagogy, could be constructed?

Drawing on case studies taken from a range of innovative secondary schools, and interrogating the use of cross-curricular approaches in UK schools, *Cross-Curricular Teaching and Learning in the Secondary School... Humanities* constructs a research-based pedagogy with practical steps for students and teachers as they consider how cross-curricular approaches can be implemented in their own subject areas.

Key features include:

- clear theoretical frameworks for cross-curricular processes of teaching and learning in the humanities;
- lively and engaging text that blends key issues with stories of current practice;
- an analysis of the use of assessment, enquiry and pupil talk as key components in building a cross-curricular approach to the humanities;
- practical and reflective tasks that enable the reader to apply their reading to day-to-day practice, alongside links to professional standards;
- summaries of key research linked to suggestions for further reading;
- professional development activities to promote cross-curricular dialogue.

Part of the *Cross-Curricular Teaching and Learning in the Secondary School* series, this timely interdisciplinary textbook is essential reading for all students on initial teacher training courses and practising teachers looking to holistically introduce cross-curricular themes and practices in secondary humanities teaching.

Richard Harris is Lecturer in History Education at the Institute of Education, University of Reading. He has chaired the Secondary Committee of the Historical Association, runs in-service training courses and acts as a consultant for various organisations, such as the Council of Europe.

Simon Harrison is Deputy Headteacher at Swanmore College of Technology. He has run training events for the Historical Association (of which he is Secondary Committee Chair), Schools History Project and the SSAT. He has also written for the journals *Teaching History* and *CPD Update*.

Richard McFahn is General Adviser for School's Support and Intervention with responsibility for Humanities. He has run numerous in-service training events for the Historical Association and is a regular workshop leader at the annual Schools History Project Conference. He is a member of the Historical Association's Secondary Committee and a member of the Geographical Association.

Cross-Curricular Teaching and Learning in ...
Series Editor – Jonathan Savage (Manchester Metropolitan University, UK)

The *Cross-Curricular* series, published by Routledge, argues for a cross-curricular approach to teaching and learning in secondary schools. It provides a justification for cross-curricularity across the Key Stages, exploring a range of theoretical and practical issues through case studies drawn from innovative practices across a range of schools. The books demonstrate the powerful nature of change that can result when teachers allow a cross-curricular 'disposition' to inspire their pedagogy. Working from a premise that there is no curriculum development without teacher development, the series argues for a serious re-engagement with cross-curricularity within the work of the individual subject teacher, before moving on to consider collaborative approaches for curriculum design and implementation through external curriculum links.

Cross-curricular approaches to teaching and learning can result in a powerful, new model of subject-based teaching and learning in the high school. This series places the teachers and their pedagogy at the centre of this innovation. The responses that schools, departments or teachers make to government initiatives in this area may only be sustainable over the short term. For longer term change to occur, models of cross-curricular teaching and learning need to become embedded within the pedagogies of individual teachers and, from there, to inform and perhaps redefine the subject cultures within which they work. These books explore how this type of change can be initiated and sustained by teachers willing to raise their heads above their 'subject' parapet and develop a broader perspective and vision for education in the 21st century.

Currently available:

Cross-Curricular Teaching and Learning in the Secondary School
By Jonathan Savage

Cross-Curricular Teaching and Learning in the Secondary School ... English
By David Stevens

Cross-Curricular Teaching and Learning in the Secondary School ... Humanities
By Richard Harris, Simon Harrison and Richard McFahn

Cross-Curricular Teaching and Learning in the Secondary School ... Mathematics
By Robert Ward-Penny

Cross-Curricular Teaching and Learning in the Secondary School... The Arts
By Martin Fautley

Forthcoming titles in the series:

Cross-Curricular Teaching and Learning in the Secondary School ... Foreign Languages
By Gee Macrory, Cathy Brady and Sheila Anthony

Cross-Curricular Teaching and Learning in the Secondary School ... Using ICT
By Maurice Nyangon

Cross-Curricular Teaching and Learning in the Secondary School ... Science
By Eleanor Brodie

CROSS-CURRICULAR TEACHING AND LEARNING IN THE SECONDARY SCHOOL

HUMANITIES

HISTORY, GEOGRAPHY, RELIGIOUS STUDIES AND CITIZENSHIP

Richard Harris, Simon Harrison and Richard McFahn

Routledge
Taylor & Francis Group

LONDON AND NEW YORK

First published 2012
by Routledge
2 Park Square, Milton Park, Abingdon, Oxon OX14 4RN

Simultaneously published in the USA and Canada
by Routledge
711 Third Avenue, New York, NY 10017

Routledge is an imprint of the Taylor & Francis Group, an informa business

British Library Cataloguing in Publication Data
A catalogue record for this book is available from the British Library

Library of Congress Cataloging in Publication Data
Harris, Richard, 1966-
Cross-curricular teaching and learning in the secondary school--- humanities : history, geography, religious studies and citizenship / Richard Harris, Simon Harrison, Richard McFahn.
p. cm. -- (Cross curricular teaching and learning in the secondary school series)
1. Education, Humanistic. 2. Humanities--Study and teaching (Secondary) 3. Citizenship--Study and teaching (Secondary) 4. Education, Secondary--Curricula. 5. Interdisciplinary approach in education. 6. Education, Secondary--Curricula--Great Britain--Case studies. 7. Interdisciplinary approach in education--Great Britain--Case studies. I. Harrison, Simon (Simon P.), 1971- II. McFahn, Richard. III. Title.
LC1011.H296 2011
370.11'2--dc23
2011021347

ISBN: 978–0–415–56188–4 (hbk)
ISBN: 978–0–415–56189–1 (pbk)
ISBN: 978–0–203–81801–5 (ebk)

Typeset in Bembo
by Saxon Graphics Ltd, Derby

Dedication

For Anna and Ruth – full of fun, curiosity and imagination! With love,

Richard

To Lindsay, Seth and Toby with love,

Si

For Jo, Archie and Harry with love,

Richard

Contents

List of figures

List of tables

List of abbreviations

AfL	assessment for learning
AST	advanced skills teacher
C Standards	core standards
GCSE	General Certificate of Secondary Education
GIS	geographic information system
HA	Historical Association
HMI	Her Majesty's Inspector
ICT	information and communication technologies
INSET	in-service education and training
IWB	interactive white board
KS	key stage
MFL	modern foreign language
NQT	newly qualified teacher
Ofsted	Office for Standards in Education
PE	physical education
PGCE	professional graduate certificate in education
PLTS	personal learning and thinking skills
PSHE	personal, social and health education
Q Standards	set of standards to qualify for the PGCE
QCA	Qualifications and Curriculum Authority
QTS	qualified teacher status
RE	religious education
RSA	Royal Society for the Encouragement of Arts, Manufactures and Commerce
SEAL	social and emotional aspects of learning
SHP	Schools' History Project
SLT	school leadership team
STEM	Science, Technology, Engineering and Mathematics

Acknowledgements

During the writing of this book we have been indebted to many individuals who have given generously of their time and expertise, and to a number of schools that have been equally generous in allowing us access to their lessons and providing opportunities to meet with staff and students. It would be invidious to mention specific individuals or institutions, as there are too many to list.

The views expressed in this book may not be shared by all those with whom we have worked. However, everyone who has been involved, in whatever form, shares a common sense of the importance of the humanities subjects as being central to the education of young people today, either as individual subjects or collectively. To that end we hope this book will further discussion and debate about the best ways in which we can help young people foster an understanding of themselves, the world in which they live and the world in which they would like to live.

1

What are the humanities and what is the context for cross-curricular teaching and learning?

Key objectives

By the end of this chapter you will have:

- explored the reasons why there has been a recent move towards greater cross-curricularity;
- explored the extent to which the subjects are similar by looking at the nature and purpose of each subject;
- compared and contrasted what is in the National Curriculum for each subject with reference to the importance statements, concepts, processes, range and breadth of content.

Teachers of the humanities subjects are generally, in our experience, very enthusiastic and passionate about their subjects. This can provoke well-intentioned rivalry between subjects, which, especially at 'options' time, can become a little more intense, as the subjects are often seen as being in competition with each other. Yet what does really separate us? As an interesting exercise, at the start of a PGCE teacher-training course, the tutors of the history, geography and RE trainees combined their groups to explore the links between the subject areas. The initial starting point however was to ask the trainees to work in their subject groups and to write down all their preconceptions and assumptions about the other subjects! This provoked much hilarity as all the stereotypes came out – we could write an entire chapter based on the outcomes, but the following just gives you a flavour of the responses: geography 'sponsored by Crayola' was a common theme amongst history and RE trainees; history was all about 'essays and dusty books' according to the geographers and RE students; whereas RE was seen as a 'doss' subject by the others! However the next task provoked a different response. This time the trainees were placed in mixed subject groups and told to talk to each other about their subjects, what they were about, why they were important and the things pupils should know and understand. This time the discussions were punctuated by lots of 'Oh, we do that as well!'

We suspect similar discussions could occur in departments and faculties in numerous other schools. Although all the authors are history teachers by training, we have worked in humanities faculties with colleagues from these other subject areas. And at times, it is clear that there are misunderstandings between teachers of different subjects.

This brief case study exemplifies these challenges.

Case study 1.1: *Richard Harris reflects on the challenges of working across the humanities subjects*

I remember clearly trying to explain an exercise using sources to two geography colleagues. The task was deceptively simple. Pupils were to be given a number of contemporary accounts of the death of Wat Tyler during the Peasants' Revolt of 1381, and would use the information from these accounts to write their own account of what happened. The problem was that the accounts differed in important details and the pupils would have to start to grapple with issues such as comparing sources, examining the provenance of the sources and so forth to create and justify the best account they could. In short it was a challenging exercise that would really force the pupils to work with evidence in a historical way. My geography colleagues nodded sagely when the task was explained to them and then asked for the 'correct' answers to help them mark the work when done. I explained to them that there was no correct answer and that pupils would have to come up with the best-reasoned answer they could, using their developing understanding of how to work with evidence. My colleagues looked at each other quizzically then looked at me and asked again for the 'correct answer' (as if I was teasing them by deliberately withholding it). It was evident that they held misconceptions about history and they did not fully understand the historical procedural knowledge the task was designed to engender. This is not to denigrate my colleagues but to illustrate the fact that, as humanities teachers, we need to understand our subjects and each other's subjects more deeply if we are to explore meaningful ways of combining the subjects to enhance the pupils' learning experience. I am sure many of my colleagues have wondered at my ignorance of geography and RE!

The focus of this chapter is to explore this issue – that is, the ways in which the humanities subjects are genuinely linked – and therefore start to explore how these links may be best exploited.

A few points of clarification

Defining what is a 'humanities' subject can be surprisingly difficult. This was seen in the early development stages of the (now defunct) 14–19 Diploma in Humanities and Social Sciences, where the number of subjects that were included within this framework varied from meeting to meeting! However, for the sake of this book, where the focus is on KS3, our attention is on those subjects which are compulsory and entail human activity at a societal level. We therefore deal with citizenship, geography, history and religious education.

We also wish to emphasise that subjects matter. Collectively the humanities matter because they are the subjects that provide the 'humane' element of the curriculum as they provide an insight into the wealth of human behaviour, and as such are an essential part of anyone's education. Individual subjects are also the basis for 'disciplined' thinking; thus it is important that the individual humanities subjects are recognisable within the curriculum. As Gardner (2007) explains, there is a difference between subject matter and discipline. Subject matter is to do with the accumulation of substantive knowledge – that is, the what, how, where, when associated with each subject area – whereas '*Disciplines* represent a radically different phenomenon. A discipline constitutes a distinctive way of thinking about the world' (Gardner, 2007: 27). This is where it becomes important that subject specialists are available to teach their subjects, as they are best placed to educate others in the ways of thinking associated with their particular disciplines. In many ways this is to be expected; subject specialists normally have greater enthusiasm for their subject areas, their subject knowledge is stronger and crucially their understanding of the subject, its nature and purpose, is more sophisticated, all of which means they are best placed to teach others.

Not all school subjects however are disciplines. History can be considered a discipline in the sense that it is a discrete subject that can be studied at degree level, and has distinctive concepts and processes which underpin the way the subject is understood (although these may be subject to dispute). A set of second order concepts has been developed in history – these shape the way we look at the past and understand it; thus cause and effect, change and continuity, chronological understanding and significance are ideas we use to create an understanding of the past. In some ways geography can also be considered a discipline. Like history it can be studied at degree level, although the subject has so many connections with other areas, such as the sciences, that many would argue it is not as distinct a discipline as history; indeed arguments about whether geography is an arts or science subject illustrate the extent of this debate (e.g. Kent, 2002). Other subjects, like citizenship, draw upon other disciplines for their knowledge and ways of working; thus citizenship is based upon subjects such as law, politics and economics, while religious education could draw upon a number of disparate fields such as sociology, theology and philosophy. Subjects which lack a disciplinary basis, like citizenship and religious education, should still be in a school curriculum as they provide important insights into human activity and are therefore worth studying, and require specialist teaching.

This presents a tension for those of us involved in education, especially at secondary school level. There are widely recognised benefits to subject-specialist teaching, but at the same time there is a growing trend towards cross-curricular approaches to teaching, which is also seen as beneficial. Gardner (2007) cites the importance of interdisciplinary thinking but raises two important caveats. Firstly, nobody can engage in interdisciplinary thinking without an understanding of the disciplines they are drawing upon to generate new meaning. Secondly, as Gardner (2007: 55) explains:

Courses may well and appropriately involve both history and the arts. One can read about the battles of the Spanish Civil War in a history text *and* one can also look at the painting *Guernica*, or read the novels of André Malraux or Ernest Hemingway, without making any particular effort to link or compare these sources. We might term this approach 'disciplinary juxtaposition' – a failure to realise the illumination that may accrue when different perspectives are synergistically joined.

The message is clear. Subjects matter, but much can be gained from bringing these together. This can only happen successfully where careful attention is paid to the value of each subject and ensuring that meaningful rather than artificial links are made between subjects.

The move towards greater cross-curricular teaching

Cross-curricular teaching is not new, but recently there has been a greater push towards this model as a means of structuring the learning experiences of young people. Although it is not the norm in schools, it is increasingly prevalent. A survey carried out by the Historical Association (Burn and Harris, 2009) found that in Year 7 approximately 85 per cent of schools continued to offer discrete subject teaching in the different humanities subjects, whilst nearly 7 per cent taught an integrated humanities programme, and a slightly larger number offered alternative curriculum approaches. The latter encompassed a vast array of programmes, such as 'Opening Minds', 'Learning to Learn', 'Building Learning Power', 'Fusion Curriculum' and so forth.

The impetus for the move towards alternative curriculum arrangements has several sources. Government agencies have been crucial in supporting schools in developing new curricular arrangements by giving them greater freedom to innovate or through new initiatives. Additionally, other interested parties have sought to offer schools support in developing new curricular programmes.

The role of government agencies and new initiatives

The introduction of the new National Curriculum in 2008 provided schools with the opportunity to adopt different approaches to the curriculum. Although coverage of subjects' content, concepts and processes is statutory, there is no obligation on schools to address this via subject teaching; instead these could be addressed through the whole-curriculum dimensions as outlined in the 'Big picture' (QCA, 2008a). Thus issues like identity and cultural diversity, community participation, the global dimension and sustainable development are supposed to permeate the curriculum and have clear links to the humanities subjects.

In addition, the focus on personalised learning and the introduction of Personal Learning and Thinking Skills (PLTS) mean that schools have been looking to provide different educational experiences for young people. The new PLTS framework emphasises the development of learners who are independent enquirers, creative thinkers, reflective learners, teamworkers, self-managers and effective participators. Clearly this could be achieved within a 'traditional' curriculum, but it does put more onuses on the process of learning, which could be radically different from what many schools currently employ.

The introduction of diplomas, with their emphasis on applied learning, has implications for teaching at KS3. Applied learning is defined as 'acquiring knowledge and skills through tasks or contexts that have many of the characteristics of real work' (QCA, 2008c: 2). The intention is that learning is grounded in 'real-life' contexts, but the inclusion of PLTS means there is a strong emphasis on the learning process and the development of particular competences. This in turn means that if schools are to embrace diplomas successfully, they must consider how they prepare students at KS3. Obviously the success and future of diplomas has yet to be settled, especially within the humanities, but their existence raises questions about how students are to be taught.

The role of other interested parties

At the same time, the development of programmes like the RSA's Opening Minds curriculum and Claxton's Building Learning Power offers schools models of practice that could be adopted. Such approaches were developed as a reaction to concerns about the growing disengagement of youngsters from education and criticisms of a curriculum that was seen as irrelevant. For example, the Opening Minds programme focuses on the development of competences within five areas: citizenship, learning, managing information, managing situations and relating to people. The emphasis is very much on understanding and doing rather than transmission of knowledge, and is designed to equip pupils with the competences that are deemed important for the twenty-first century. Again, as with PLTS, there is an emphasis on the process of learning rather than what is learned. These competences are developed through units of work, which are designed to ensure the statutory elements of the National Curriculum are met. Understanding how well these approaches work is important, because according to the RSA's own 2008 impact report, most schools adopt a competency model within the humanities subjects. This report (admittedly a very self-interested one) claims that such approaches have a major positive impact on pupils' experience of education and their attainment. There does seem to be some merit in what such courses are able to achieve, but this does not mean they are universally successful. A recent Ofsted (2009a) report provides an evaluation of the impact of the new KS3 curriculum, including the development of competency-based courses. Although they recognised many benefits

> subject inspectors also identified emerging problems with the courses. These included the loss of subject content and subject skills development; lack of continuity from primary school experience; lack of rigour and challenge; uneven quality of teaching and artificial 'links' or themes. These problems were especially manifested where courses had been given insufficient planning time and where the component subject departments were not fully involved in planning.
>
> (Ofsted, 2009: 12).

Summary

It is clear that there has been greater attention recently on the development of cross-curricular courses, and that in many schools the humanities is seen as an appropriate area to support such a move. Similarly a focus on the process of learning is also to be welcomed, as are attempts to make pupils see the value of their learning. However this should not be at the expense of hindering young people's understanding of the separate subject areas. Different subjects have different modes of thinking and procedures, which are part of the subject discipline. It is also important that young people receive a coherent educational experience; indeed one of the major pushes in recent history teaching has been the need to provide students with a coherent framework of the past, and so any attempt to offer a cross-curricular approach to learning about the past raises potential additional obstacles in meeting this aim. The emphasis on cross-curricular approaches that focus on the process of learning also runs the risk of denigrating the importance of subject content. It is easy to dismiss content as irrelevant and outmoded but the development of any curricular model is a political act. What is included matters (and by default what is excluded).

Thus the concerns raised within the recent Ofsted (2009a) report have to be taken seriously. It is appropriate to take into account the process of learning but there needs to be a coherent approach which develops an understanding of the different subject disciplines within the humanities and provides progression for aspects such as PLTS and subject-specific concepts and processes, as well as ensuring that the choice of content is appropriate and not simply coincidental.

It is at this point that it should be clear that any successful move towards greater cross-curricularity depends on the individual development of teachers. Organisational issues in schools, such as decisions about curriculum construction (i.e. based on subjects, themes and so forth), may be more or less supportive of teachers' attempts to adopt a cross-curricular way of working, but little impact will be made unless teachers themselves attempt to understand the other subject areas and identify ways in which they can draw on these within their own practice. This is an issue that is highlighted in the introductory book to this series (Savage, 2011). The rest of this chapter explores the nature and purpose of the humanities subjects in order to help individual teachers better understand what the 'other' subjects are about, and therefore to reflect on the ways in which individual teachers can draw upon them to enhance their personal pedagogy and the experiences of their pupils.

What are the similarities and differences between the different humanities subjects?

As the RSA's (2008) impact report highlights, many schools use the humanities as a means of introducing the Opening Minds curriculum, and there has long been a tradition of schools which teach humanities or arrange teaching within a humanities faculty. This often requires teachers to teach outside their subject areas; indeed, all of us at different stages in our careers have had to teach outside our specialisms. To an extent this is understandable, but at the same time it is highly unlikely that any of us would have been asked to teach maths or science because these are such different subjects, yet there is a common-sense assumption that the connections between the humanities subjects are so close that specialist understanding is not necessary. Yet, having all worked in humanities faculties, we can recognise the difficulties our teams had in understanding aspects of other subjects and the important nuances of different tasks, or why certain topics were considered essential to the subject.

It is clear that in order for any cross-curricular humanities work to be successful there is a need for teachers from different subject backgrounds to appreciate more fully the nature of the different subjects, how they organise knowledge and understanding and how they operate as subjects. This section will therefore provide an outline of key developments and debates within the humanities subjects so as to allow colleagues from different backgrounds to better understand the issues inherent in each subject area. It will then compare and contrast the National Curriculum for each subject to examine what makes each subject distinctive and where there is genuine opportunity for collaborative work.

Debates and developments in the nature and purpose of the humanities subjects

Citizenship

As a school subject, citizenship is a relative newcomer in the UK. There have been earlier attempts to provide some form of citizenship education, but these have been influenced by different notions of citizenship. Broadly speaking, there are two main conceptions of citizenship, namely the civic republican ideal and the liberal tradition. There is insufficient space here to do justice to these differing concepts of citizenship (a fuller discussion can be found in Heater, 1999), so what follows is a necessarily a simplified discussion. An essential difference between the civic and liberal concepts of citizenship concerns the role and relationship of the state and the individual. In the civic republican tradition, the well-being of the state is predominant, and the role of the individual is to look at ways they can serve the community. There is thus an emphasis on duties. In the liberal tradition there is a greater emphasis on individual rights, with looser ties to the state, though there is a need to promote democratic values if liberal democracy is to thrive.

Though the civic republican model has its origins in Ancient Greece and has thus been with us for a considerable period of time, it is the relative newcomer, the liberal tradition, that generally holds sway in the contemporary world. However as states develop, so does the nature of being a citizen within the state, and it is this that makes citizenship a complex subject. To be an effective citizen in either model (no matter what type of state exists) requires some form of education. Heater (1999: 164) argues that:

> Citizens need knowledge and understanding of the social, legal and political system(s) in which they live and operate. They need skills and aptitudes to make use of that knowledge and understanding. And they need to be endowed with values and dispositions to put their knowledge and skills to beneficial use.

This is a useful definition, and echoes that of T.H. Marshall who emphasised civil (largely property rights), social (mainly welfare rights) and participatory rights (via voting).

Although citizenship was a non-statutory element of the first National Curriculum, it had little impact on the school curriculum. Following the review of the National Curriculum in 1995, a 'Forum on Values in Education and the Community' was set up to review several aspects of the curriculum, including the citizenship component, but its 'Statement of values' in 1997 again had little discernible impact on schools. However the election of New Labour in 1997 brought a greater imperative to the debate about citizenship education. A working group under the direction of Bernard Crick produced an influential report in 1998 and argued that 'Citizenship education is an unfulfilled

7

expectation in a national agenda' (QCA, 1998: 8) and, given strong political backing, this report was translated into a new curriculum subject. Citizenship education was to become statutory in 2002, although it was introduced in 2000 so as to give schools a two-year period to prepare for its implementation. This highlights the seriousness with which the government at the time perceived the subject. This citizenship curriculum was loosely based upon the ideas of political literacy, social and moral responsibility, and community involvement (though the document as written did not use these terms, it was based upon these ideas). Political literacy was seen as essential in engaging young people in action, whilst community involvement envisaged more voluntary activity. The social and moral responsibility strand was to foster desirable values, and emphasised responsibilities as well as rights. Within the actual curriculum these ideas were translated into knowledge and understanding about becoming informed citizens, developing skills of enquiry and communication, and participation and taking responsible action. All three strands were interconnected. The latter strand was probably the most interesting, implying that schools had to educate pupils to become active citizens 'where pupils learn the knowledge citizens need through taking part in activities that generate it' (Keast, 2003: 33).

However the subject has been the focus of much scrutiny and debate. The Ofsted report (2006) *Towards Consensus?* shows that although progress has been made in its implementation there is still much that needs to be done for the subject to be properly embedded in the curriculum. In some schools there is little understanding of or support for it. To an extent this is understandable given the complexities of the subject. There are practical considerations such as preparing teachers to teach citizenship, concerns about how to promote active participation, the extent to which teachers are prepared to teach a subject with such explicit values and so forth. The more recent Ofsted report (2010a) *Citizenship Established?* indicates that, although there are continuing improvements, these concerns persist.

There are some who argue more fundamentally that citizenship is not a subject of study but an outcome of education. For example Pring (2006: 58) argues:

> The nurturing of future citizens – the development of the virtues and modes of understanding which characterise good citizenship – is intrinsic to the process of helping young people to become human, and to live actively and constructively within an enriching community. Citizenship may not be the word used, but the educated person should be a good citizen by virtue of his being educated.

Others have attacked the model of citizenship put forward within the curriculum. For example, Faulks (2006) has criticised the idea of political literacy. He rightly claims that citizenship is a contested notion but that this does not appear within the curriculum, and so argues there is an emphasis on encouraging participation in the political process rather than questioning or challenging how the process operates. If the purpose of citizenship education is to promote 'active' participation, then questions about the current status quo in society need to be raised, drawing on the past to explain how the situation has arisen but also provoking debate about what it could be like.

Another critic of the original citizenship curriculum is Kiwan (2008). She highlights two particular weaknesses. She agrees that citizenship has a moral angle to it, but feels the Crick Report emphasised moral values as generating respect for existing institutions and the rule of law and overlooked the development of personal values. Although the National Curriculum does mention personal values, it is not clear how these are supposed to operate in a public or political sphere (to an extent this is due to the separation of citizenship and PSHE, which nevertheless creates blurred boundaries). For example, there has been much talk about 'shared values' and 'Britishness', but what if these values (however they are defined) are in conflict with personally held beliefs? For example, Britain is effectively a secular nation state. Consequently there is a relationship between the individual and the state, which may manifest itself in some form of patriotism or loyalty to the state, and the state in turn has responsibilities to its citizens. But what happens if an individual's personal values and those of the state are in conflict? For example, current British foreign policy means the country has a military commitment in Iraq and Afghanistan, but what if you are a pacifist and object to such commitments or are a British Muslim and see such involvement as an attack on your religious identity. Kiwan also argues that citizenship is to do with the development of identity (which is defined in very broad terms), which is absent from the original curriculum. Individuals are able to hold multiple identities, depending on context, and citizenship can help young people foster this awareness.

More recently, the Ajegbo report (DfES, 2007) has added another element to the citizenship agenda. Thus identity has become an important element within the curriculum, and history is seen as an additional strand within citizenship that contributes to an understanding of identity. In part this is due to a different conceptualisation of citizenship from that of the Crick report, and in part to the different social and political contexts (1998 and 2007) in which the two reports were written. The Crick report emerged at a time of concerns about political apathy, whereas the Ajegbo report emerged in an era of concerns about 'home-grown' terrorism and fears of a breakdown in society. In turn this suggests that citizenship, as a school subject, is very open to political and social pressures. In many ways this is unsurprising given the contemporary nature of the subject, but it also emphasises the importance of the subject and that pupils need to understand that it is a contested subject.

Geography

The development of geography as a school subject has seen numerous changes, which have pulled the subject in different directions and reflect debates about the nature and purpose of the subject. To an extent this is related to the fact that there are human and physical dimensions to the study of geography, both of which can be studied in different ways. Consequently there are debates about the nature of geography and whether it is at heart a subject based in science, the arts or the social sciences. Such debates in turn influence the nature and purpose of school geography.

In the earlier days of geography teaching there was an emphasis on what has been termed the 'capes and bays' approach, which essentially focused on the transmission of knowledge about places and geographical features. In addition, much geography teaching in the 1960s through to the 1980s focused on regional and/or physical geography (see Lambert and Balderstone, 2010). These approaches put the main educational emphasis on transmission of cultural heritage, where hopefully the intrinsic appeal of the subject is apparent and pupils are inspired by the awe and wonder of the world in which they live. Potentially such an approach can provide opportunities for fieldwork investigations and enquiry approaches to learning but it can easily lapse into the mere acquisition of factual knowledge, which educationally has its limitations.

However, developments within geography amongst researchers brought a change of direction in school geography teaching. 'New' geography emerged during the 1960s and 1970s, based upon a more scientific approach to the subject. In this mode, geography was seen as a much more theoretical subject, involving a search for general laws that could be used to explain a range of geographical phenomenon, for example the study of spatial processes and patterns to explain human settlement. Although this readily applied to human geography it could also apply to aspects of physical geography, such as the study of rivers. Within schools this meant a greater emphasis on using data collection and hypothesis testing. It was an attack on regional geography, which was seen as focusing on the unique features of a locality rather than more 'scientific' and generalisable rules which would provide more explanatory power for geography.

Further developments were prompted by different projects like Geography for the Young School Leaver (a Schools' Council project which led to the development of the Avery Hill specification) and the Bristol Project (which also formed the basis of a GCSE specification). Both of these were teacher led and had a stronger focus on skills, and topics and issues that would be more appealing to pupils. These developments combined elements of the 'new' geography, with its emphasis on spatial awareness, with better understanding of social issues; thus industrial development could be studied in the context of unemployment patterns. The emergence of environmental concerns in the late 1980s has also impacted on the curriculum, by bringing a greater concern for social issues and values-based education into the subject.

The introduction of the first National Curriculum in 1988 created a curriculum with which many were unhappy, focusing more on content knowledge than skills development, and was heavily assessment driven with five attainment targets. Subsequent revisions to the curriculum have reduced the content requirement and emphasised more the development of skills necessary for investigation and enquiry.

Kent (2002) outlines the general developments in geography teaching by showing how fieldwork has developed, in which the different traditions of geography teaching can be seen. Initially, field teaching or excursions were designed to 'read' the environment; thus a knowledgeable expert would explain the features of a location, whilst students took notes, made sketches and answered questions. Later came hypothesis testing, drawing on the scientific approach of the 'new' geography. Here the focus was on gathering data, often of a statistical nature, to test a hypothesis. The other development was in 'framework fieldwork'. Here issues or problems were identified for study which had a people–environment focus. There was a strong emphasis on enquiry into an issue which was often value laden.

School geography can therefore be seen as meeting several different purposes. At one level it is about the development of skills, both subject specific and generic. These include literacy, numeracy, graphicacy and ICT, which can lead to the development of functionally literate individuals who can contribute to the workplace. Geography is also seen as possessing great cultural capital, with its subject matter being of high intrinsic interest and value. It can be argued that individuals need a strong sense of place and understanding of the physical and natural world in which they live in order to make sense of the contemporary world. Geography can also be seen as developing a strong social and political awareness of important issues facing humanity, and therefore provides a vehicle for developing values and commitment to social action.

None of these positions are mutually exclusive, but it is important to reflect on your own understanding of geography and your sense of its purpose, as these will influence how the subject is taught and what is taught.

History

Like geography, history has undergone several changes in the nature and purpose of what pupils study. History teaching, as Sylvester explains, used to be dominated by the 'Great Tradition'. Sylvester (1994: 9) observes:

> The history teacher's role was didactically active; it was to give pupils the facts of historical knowledge and to ensure, through repeated short tests, that they had learned them. The pupil's role was passive: history was a 'received subject'. The body of knowledge to be taught was also clearly defined. It was mainly political history with some social and economic aspects, and it was mainly British history, with some European, from Julius Caesar to 1914.

The purpose of this curriculum was relatively straightforward. History was being studied both for its intrinsic value and to develop an assumed shared cultural heritage, which posited a progressive view of Britain's past towards greater democracy and improving social welfare. This tradition did not go unchallenged; for example Keatinge in 1910 proposed a style of teaching based upon the use of historical evidence, and in 1928 Happold suggested a more active approach to teaching and learning, but the 'Great Tradition' remained the dominant form for the best part of the twentieth century. A great deal of teaching history was based upon a mis-assumption about what children were capable of doing.

Real change emerged from the 1960s. Price's (1968) critique of history teaching is often cited as pivotal in precipitating a change, but the 1960s were a period in which there was a great deal of educational experimentation, much of it fostered by the Schools' Council. Most significantly the Schools' Council funded a history project in 1972. This project, commonly known as the Schools' History Project (SHP) was to prove hugely influential in developing history education. It differed from more traditional teaching approaches by emphasising a conceptual and procedural approach to history teaching. This meant that pupils were to learn about how historians find out about the past through the use of evidence, whilst also developing an understanding of historical concepts like causation and change and continuity. Part of the process was to help pupils understand how history was constructed. Additionally the SHP approach focused on different subject matter. There was an emphasis on different types of history; thus local history, contemporary history, depth studies and development studies were to become part of this approach.

Interestingly the project's starting point focused on the perceived needs of young people and tried to construct a curriculum around that. It also challenged much thinking, derived from Piaget, that most young people struggled with abstract concepts and therefore suggested history teaching ought to focus on teaching the concrete facts of the past. In that sense it was able to liberate teachers from an emphasis on the grind through from 'Plato to Nato'.

The influence of the SHP has been extensive. Its focus on concepts and processes of history can be seen in the various developments of the National Curriculum. These concepts and processes have proved relatively stable through the different manifestations of the curriculum and are central to an understanding of progression within the subject; they may occasionally be repackaged but there has been a strong continuity from 1990. Where the National Curriculum versions of history have changed most is in relation to the content and periods to be studied. The initial version of the curriculum was seen as content heavy, with units having to be taught in chronological order. Subsequent versions of the curriculum have gradually reduced the burden of content but the content was still explained in periods of time that had to be studied. The most recent version of the curriculum has moved away from this by devising a series of themes that need to be explored.

The SHP is also unusual in developing an examination course derived from its core principles and philosophy, requiring pupils to work with evidence and to carry out fieldwork in the locality. The introduction of GCSEs in the 1980s also saw the influence of the SHP. The new assessment objectives required pupils to develop an understanding of key concepts like cause and consequence and the ability to work with a range of historical evidence.

The teaching of history has therefore moved a long way from ideas of teaching facts and dates, to an emphasis on the process of studying history and understanding that history is a construct, and thus is open to interpretation, where multiple perspectives are valid. The reasons for teaching history have therefore also undergone a transformation. No longer is the emphasis on developing a shared sense of a common heritage or promoting some form of patriotism. History is seen as important in developing a sense of identity and helping young people understand the world in which they live. The extent to which the past 'teaches' us lessons for today is highly dubious, and there are arguments within the history community about the extent to which history enables students to engage with moral issues, but there are strong arguments (e.g. Barton and Levstik, 2004; Tosh, 2008) for history's role in supporting liberal democratic thinking. Other arguments put forward by Rüsen (2004) stress the value of 'historical consciousness', whereby our understanding of the past influences how we see the present and therefore shapes what we see as possible future actions.

Again, it is important to reflect upon your understanding of the nature and purpose of history, so that you are better able to understand why the subject matters, and consequently what should be taught.

Religious education

In many ways the status of RE is similar to that of citizenship, although within the National Curriculum RE does not have a statutory programme of study. As Rudge (2000) points out, RE has an unusual position within the curriculum, being at the same time compulsory and optional (as pupils can be withdrawn), and also having a national framework but one which is decided locally.

As with the other humanities subjects, RE has been subject to much debate regarding its purpose. Rudge (2000) outlines three general aims of RE: induction into a community or culture, a liberal study of religion, and as an agent of humanisation. Thus to some , subject is about nurturing someone into a particular faith; for others it is the opportunity to draw upon knowledge and understanding of religion to make informed judgements on sensitive and controversial issues; or it could be about enabling the spiritual development of young people to develop their sense of identity and their views on issues such as justice and respect. As such RE can be regarded as an academic subject to develop an understanding of the world based upon knowledge of religions, it can be used to promote personal development through reflection on beliefs and values, it can promote critical thinking, encourage dialogue between people of different beliefs and it can get pupils to ask ultimate questions about life and humanity. This range of aims is reflected in Grimmit's (2000) study where he examines eight different pedagogical approaches to RE, each influenced by a different purpose.

This range of ideas can be seen in the non-statutory guidance (QCA/DfES, 2004) which was produced to provide additional guidance for teachers. Within the breadth of study, students were to learn about major religions, one of which had to be Christianity. They were also to examine a range of themes, such as beliefs and concepts, authority, religion and science, ethics and relationships. Students were also to have experiences and opportunities, which would cover visits to places of religious significance, encountering people from other faiths, opportunities to discuss issues and reflect upon their personal values and beliefs, as well as those of others. The guidance effectively set out the type of knowledge that students were expected to acquire and stressed the development of particular dispositions and ways of thinking. The curriculum also stressed the importance of learning about and learning from religion.

Learning about religion implies that the focus is on acquisition of knowledge about religion(s), such as knowledge of specific rituals and symbols. This can lead to a very narrow curriculum which, although easy to assess, is unlikely to contribute much to pupils' understanding of themselves or the world in which they live. Learning from religion has a completely different emphasis. The focus is on understanding the beliefs of others, which in turn has the potential to clarify one's own beliefs. It is designed to be 'mind opening', getting individuals to focus on their values and appreciate the values of others, whilst at the same time posing fundamental questions about the human condition. Unfortunately too much RE teaching appears to be focused on learning about religion rather than learning from religion; the recent Ofsted (2007) report claims that too much teaching at KS3 is unchallenging.

Reflective task 1.1

Drawing on the preceding sections about the subject areas, what are the key debates within each subject area and how do these impact on the way the subject should be taught? How similar are these debates? How might these debates help or hinder cross-curricular teaching? What issues does this present for staff teaching outside their subject area and what can be done to support these staff?

Curriculum

:ion the different programmes of study will be examined to highlight ind differences between these four subject areas. The reason for doing this is one level it will help to pinpoint the distinctiveness of each subject, so that sts are better able to appreciate what they are striving to achieve within these different areas. In addition, an examination of the similarities across the subjects will help to identify opportunities for meaningful cross-curricular work.

The importance statements

It may be an obvious statement but the importance statements are important! Such statements existed in previous versions of the National Curriculum, but they were widely ignored . Within the new National Curriculum these statements are there to clarify what is the value of the different subjects in a young person's education, and they are designed to provide a rationale for the concepts, processes and content that are contained in the programmes of study. They provide a central pillar in the thinking behind the curriculum as all other aspects contained within the documents – that is, concepts, processes, range and breadth of content – are supposed to stem from these importance statements. By comparing the statements (Table 1.1) it is possible to look for areas of commonality, which in turn can be used to create a rationale for creating any cross-curricular work.

Table 1.1 National Curriculum importance statements for the humanities subjects

Citizenship	Geography

Education for citizenship equips young people with the knowledge, skills and understanding to play an effective role in public life. Citizenship encourages them to take an interest in topical and controversial issues and to engage in discussion and debate. Pupils learn about their rights, responsibilities, duties and freedoms, and about laws, justice and democracy. They learn to take part in decision making and different forms of action. They play an active role in the life of their schools, neighbourhoods, communities and wider society as active and global citizens.
 	
  Citizenship encourages respect for different national, religious and ethnic identities. It equips pupils to engage critically with and explore diverse ideas, beliefs, cultures and identities, and the values we share as citizens in the UK. Pupils begin to understand how society has changed and is
	The study of geography stimulates an interest in and a sense of wonder about places. It helps young people make sense of a complex and dynamically changing world. It explains where places are, how places and landscapes are formed, how people and their environment interact, and how a diverse range of economies, societies and environments are interconnected. It builds on pupils' own experiences to investigate places at all scales, from the personal to the global.
	
	  Geographical enquiry encourages questioning, investigation and critical thinking about issues affecting the world and people's lives, now and in the future. Fieldwork is an essential element of this. Pupils learn to think spatially and use maps, visual images and new technologies, including geographical information systems (GIS), to obtain, present and analyse information. Geography inspires pupils to

Citizenship (cont.)	Geography (cont.)
changing in the UK, Europe and the wider world. Citizenship addresses issues relating to social justice, human rights, community cohesion and global interdependence, and encourages pupils to challenge injustice, inequalities and discrimination. It helps young people to develop their critical skills, consider a wide range of political, social, ethical and moral problems, and explore opinions and ideas other than their own. They evaluate information, make informed judgements and reflect on the consequences of their actions now and in the future. They learn to argue a case on behalf of others as well as themselves and speak out on issues of concern. Citizenship equips pupils with the knowledge and skills needed for effective and democratic participation. It helps pupils to become informed, critical, active citizens who have the confidence and conviction to work collaboratively, take action and try to make a difference in their communities and the wider world.	become global citizens by exploring their own place in the world, their values and their responsibilities to other people, to the environment and to the sustainability of the planet.
History	**RE**
History fires pupils' curiosity and imagination, moving and inspiring them with the dilemmas, choices and beliefs of people in the past. It helps pupils develop their own identities through an understanding of history at personal, local, national and international levels. It helps them to ask and answer questions of the present by engaging with the past. Pupils find out about the history of their community, Britain, Europe and the world. They develop a chronological overview that enables them to make connections within and across different periods and societies. They investigate Britain's relationships with the wider world, and relate past events to the present day.	RE provokes challenging questions about the ultimate meaning and purpose of life, beliefs about God, the self and the nature of reality, issues of right and wrong and what it means to be human. It develops pupils' knowledge and understanding of Christianity, other principal religions, other religious traditions, and other world views that offer answers to these challenging questions. It offers opportunities for personal reflection and spiritual development. It enhances pupils' awareness and understanding of religions and beliefs, teachings, practices and forms of expression, as well as of the influence of religion on individuals, families, communities and cultures.

History (cont.)	**RE** (cont.)
As they develop their understanding of the nature of historical study, pupils ask and answer important questions, evaluate evidence, identify and analyse different interpretations of the past, and learn to substantiate any arguments and judgements they make. They appreciate why they are learning what they are learning and can debate its significance. History prepares pupils for the future, equipping them with knowledge and skills that are prized in adult life, enhancing employability and developing an ability to take part in a democratic society. It encourages mutual understanding of the historic origins of our ethnic and cultural diversity, and helps pupils become confident and questioning individuals.	RE encourages pupils to learn from different religions, beliefs, values and traditions, while exploring their own beliefs and questions of meaning. It challenges pupils to reflect on, consider, analyse, interpret and evaluate issues of truth, belief, faith and ethics, and to communicate their responses. RE encourages pupils to develop their sense of identity and belonging. It enables them to flourish individually within their communities and as citizens in a diverse society and global community. RE has an important role in preparing pupils for adult life, employment and lifelong learning. It enables pupils to develop respect for and sensitivity to others, in particular those whose faiths and beliefs are different from their own. It promotes discernment and enables pupils to combat prejudice.

Looking at these importance statements, several things stand out which link the subjects. As the subjects are all to do with human activity there is an emphasis on understanding ourselves and 'others', and being able to fit into and contribute to society. Issues of personal identity are particularly prominent in the history and RE statements and are implicit in the citizenship one, but all four explicitly refer to the need to examine the views of others and the interconnectedness of society, and to appreciate the rich diversity of society. In relation to this the statements also indicate that the subject areas are trying to promote particular attitudes and dispositions, although this varies in emphasis. Citizenship clearly promotes the idea of responsibilities and the need to take informed action to make a difference, whilst in geography there is an emphasis on young people exploring their place in the world and addressing their responsibilities as global citizens. This point is made specifically in relation to environmental issues, but is nonetheless expressing the view that as a result of a geographical education young people are, it is hoped, to take responsibility for the consequences of their actions. The RE statement is also very explicit in its assumption that the subject will develop respect and tolerance for others, and will enable pupils to counter prejudice. The idea of developing specific attitudes is more understated in the history curriculum, but there is still a reference to encouraging mutual understanding, implying that tolerance will be an outcome of a historical education. An anticipated outcome of an education in these subjects is the assumption that students will be able to participate in and contribute to a diverse and democratic society. Thus all the statements talk about helping young people understand the world in which they live and have the knowledge and skills to make an effective contribution to society, but this is also where differences become apparent.

To understand the world in which they live, young people need to have knowledge of the world, yet each subject brings a different understanding of knowledge, both substantive and syntactic. This will be dealt with more fully when analysing the concepts, processes, and range and breadth of content for the subjects, but in brief, in citizenship the substantive knowledge is very much about rights and responsibilities and the decision-making processes that happen, as well as topical events. The need to focus on current events may well overlap with the other subject areas; for example, many environmental issues will fall easily into a citizenship or geographical context. But there are major differences in the 'bread and butter' content of the subject areas; although history is as much about the present as the past, it illuminates the present by looking at the past; geography focuses on place, landscapes and environments (both human and physical); while RE is about beliefs, values and religious practices. There is also a danger that simplistic cross-curricular links can distort the subjects. For example it is possible to make strong links between history and citizenship, but because citizenship is about 'now', identifying historical topics to support an understanding of a current issue, although possible and desirable in many ways, can lead to a 'presentist' approach to the past; in other words the only bits of the past that are deemed worthy of study are those that have an immediate relevance to the current situation, which would restrict the scope of what is studied and therefore serve to limit a student's understanding of the past.

Similarly, although it would be possible to make common-sense assumptions about the syntactic knowledge that underpins the subjects, such as causation in history or sense of place in geography, there are distinct ways of thinking about such concepts which can only be taught with a thorough understanding of the particular subject or discipline. It is therefore vitally important that any cross-curricular approaches to teaching these subjects is based upon a clear understanding of the subject areas and the thinking and discipline that underpins these.

Practical task 1.1

What would an importance statement look like for the humanities? Note down some ideas about what could be included in it. How easy is it to do this? What would you be 'losing' from your own subject in creating this? What clear common ground emerges? This will get you thinking about where the benefits of working across the humanities might be, and where the compromises lie. How easy did you find this to do?

Concepts and processes

The most recent National Curriculum follows a common format, which is helpful in identifying ways in which the subjects are similar but also helps to emphasise how they are different. It is extremely important to take this into consideration when designing any cross-curricular work so as to ensure that the different elements of the subjects are being genuinely covered.

The concepts (Table 1.2) that underpin the subjects are crucial as they provide the structure which shapes the way we think about the subject and therefore the type of

Table 1.2 Concepts specified in the National Curriculum for the humanities subjects

Citizenship	Geography
Democracy and justice Rights and responsibilities Identities and diversity: living together in the UK	Place Space Scale Interdependence Physical and human processes Environmental interaction and sustainable development Cultural understanding and diversity
History	**RE**
Chronological understanding Cultural, ethnic and religious diversity Change and continuity Cause and consequence Significance Interpretation	Beliefs, teachings and sources Practices and ways of life Expressive meaning Identity, diversity and belonging Meaning, purpose and truth Values and commitment

thinking that students need to be engaged with. The concepts that shape the humanities subjects are largely distinct from each other, and it is therefore difficult to argue that conceptual links between the subjects should form the basis of any joint work. Instead the subjects would bring different ways of thinking when focused on a concept. Looking at the concepts holistically also highlights different emphases of the subjects. Both citizenship and RE have a greater focus on values, attitudes, beliefs and dispositions, whereas history and geography employ concepts that reflect the types of thinking that shape the way the subjects are understood.

An obvious area where there appears to be a strong connection is the area of identity and diversity. History can provide a context for exploring diversity through a study of migration, with a focus on similarity and difference between the experiences of a wide range of people. This would also largely satisfy the citizenship requirements for this concept. To an extent such a historical context could satisfy some elements of the geographical elements of cultural understanding and diversity, although within a geography context there is a stronger focus on the 'here and now'. In RE the focus is on the role of faith and beliefs in developing a sense of identity.

It is possible to take a concept from one subject and see where it appears elsewhere. For example, if you take a concept like change and continuity in history, it is possible to see connections in geography's ideas about place, space and physical and human processes. In terms of place and space students are expected to understand how things changed, whilst also exploring the physical and human processes that bring about change. What needs to be borne in mind, though, is the different types of thinking that each subject would wish to develop. For example history and geography teachers would probably both be interested in identifying trends and patterns, as well as categorising the types of change and evaluating the significance of different factors that lead to change.

However geographers may be focused on social, economic and environmental change, and wish to explore past, present and future trends, whereas a history teacher may focus on the past but look more broadly at the concept of change, and so a history teacher may be more likely to want students to explore ideas about the rate of change or to examine potential turning points and so forth. It is less easy to discern a similar focus in either RE or citizenship.

Although RE and citizenship do have a more values-based approach to the concepts, the connections between the two subject areas are not that clear. For example, RE addresses values and commitments, whilst citizenship looks at rights and responsibilities; and although both deal with how people should act, in RE the focus is on the way that moral values are derived from beliefs and experience and how this influences decision making, whereas in citizenship the emphasis is on rights and responsibilities from a political, legal, human, social, civic and moral standpoint, the impact of these on people, how to safeguard and promote them, and the tensions that they create.

Beyond these conceptual links it becomes increasingly difficult to identify areas that offer genuine opportunities to make connections across the subjects.

Whereas the concepts outline the types of thinking that shape the subjects, the processes (Table 1.3) focus on how the subjects 'work': that is, how knowledge is generated or the actions required to make the subjects happen. It is much easier to find procedural commonalities rather than conceptual ones across the humanities, although there are differences which highlight the fundamental nature of the subjects.

Table 1.3 Processes specified in the National Curriculum for the humanities subjects

Citizenship	Geography
Critical thinking and enquiry Advocacy and representation Taking informed and responsible action	Geographical enquiry Fieldwork and out-of-class learning Graphicacy and visual literacy Geographical communication
History	RE
Historical enquiry Using evidence Communicating about the past	Learning about religion Learning from religion

Enquiry is part of citizenship, geography and history. In these three areas, students are expected to plan enquiries, which include identifying areas to investigate, gathering data or information, and analysing the information critically. Having gone through this process students are expected to be able to present views that are grounded in the evidence and can be justified. Differences are apparent, though, in the field of study. History is self-evidently rooted in the past, whilst in geography topics are more likely to be environmental or based around contemporary issues, and it is expected that fieldwork will be included in some elements of enquiry. Citizenship is different in the requirement to focus on topical and controversial issues, and more importantly, emphasises the need for social action; having learnt about an issue there is an expectation that students are to take informed action and reflect upon the process of taking such action, which may well include the process of working with others or an analysis of the impact of any actions. In all three areas there is a clear expectation that students will be helped to become independent learners. The processes highlighted in RE are of a different nature; although students may well be expected to carry out an enquiry, the process is characterised more by a personal, reflective response rather than a critical appraisal of knowledge and supporting evidence. Thus students are generally expected to investigate, evaluate and analyse beliefs and values (either their own or from other systems of beliefs), and to reflect on and express the insights these provide into a range of issues. Overall the processes in RE appear to require more reflective work from students. These differences, and the ways in which they can be approached, will be explored in greater depth in Chapter 4.

Despite the considerable overlap in terms of processes, these alone are unlikely to form a suitable means of establishing cross-curricular links, because a focus on generic processes is relatively meaningless without a specific context – skills are best developed when learning about something specific, and in this sense are best developed through some subject-specific content. With that in mind, we need to look more closely at the 'range and content' for each subject (Table 1.4).

Range and content

As part of the review of the National Curriculum, working groups were asked to remove specific content from the programmes of study so as to allow schools greater freedom in planning their curricula. Given this requirement it is surprising that the history curriculum had content rewritten back into it despite the efforts of the working group to remove this element. Consequently, history ended up with more required content than it previously had! All the programmes of study, though, provide flexibility, which can be used intelligently to make connections across the subjects.

Connections between the subjects are, on the surface, rather limited. Both history and citizenship share a focus on the development of the UK and migration. Migration is not specifically mentioned in the geography headings but would undoubtedly form part of the study of human geography. Although not specifically mentioned in the RE curriculum, it is possible to see how the development of a multi-faith society through migration could form a topic for investigation. Citizenship, geography and history also require a study of the role of the European Union and other such institutions. In history, the development of political power would form the context for citizenship's focus on parliamentary democracy and the development of political, legal and human rights, which in turn could feed into RE and discussions about ethics, and rights and responsibilities. All four subjects also offer the scope to explore global issues such as the environment or conflict resolution.

However it needs to be borne in mind that the subject matter of each area is different and that, instead of looking for areas of commonality per se, it is important to consider what is distinctive about each subject and what knowledge and understanding each can bring to an area of study. For example, the geography programme of study outlines the need for investigations, including those of places, but to make this the focus of interesting cross-curricular work requires some lateral thinking. In this case, the idea of place raises

Table 1.4 Range and breadth of content specified in the National Curriculum for the humanities subjects

Citizenship	Geography
The study of citizenship should include:	**The study of geography should include:**
a. Political, legal and human rights, and responsibilities of citizens.	a. A variety of scales, from personal, local, regional, national, international and continental, to global.
b. The roles of the law and the justice system and how they relate to young people.	b. A range of investigations, focusing on places, themes or issues.
c. Key features of parliamentary democracy and government in the constituent parts of the UK and at local level, including voting and elections.	c. The location of places and environments.
	d. Key aspects of the UK, including its changing human and physical geography, current issues and its place in the world today.
d. Freedom of speech and diversity of views, and the role of the media in informing and influencing public opinion and holding those in power to account.	e. Different parts of the world in their wider settings and contexts, including the European Union and regions or countries in different states of development.
e. Actions that individuals, groups and organisations can take to influence decisions affecting communities and the environment.	f. Physical geography, physical processes and natural landscapes.
f. Strategies for handling local and national disagreements and conflicts.	g. Human geography, built and managed environments, and human processes.
g. The needs of the local community and how these are met through public services and the voluntary sector.	h. Interactions between people and their environments, including causes and consequences of these interactions, and how to plan for and manage their future impact.
h. How economic decisions are made, including where public money comes from and who decides how it is spent.	
i. The changing nature of UK society, including the diversity of ideas, beliefs, cultures, identities, traditions, perspectives and values that are shared.	
j. Migration to, from and within the UK and the reasons for this.	
k. The UK's relations with the European Union and the rest of Europe, the Commonwealth, the United Nations and the world as a global community.	

History	RE
The study of history should be taught through a combination of overview, thematic and depth studies.	**The study of RE should include:**
a. In order to give pupils a secure chronological framework, the choice of content should ensure that all pupils can identify and understand the major events, changes and developments in British, European and world history, covering at least the medieval, early modern, industrial and twentieth-century periods. b. Appropriate links should be made to some of the parallel events, changes and developments in British, European and world history. c. Within these broad parameters, all pupils should be taught aspects of history, including:	a. Christianity. b. At least two other principal religions. c. A religious community of local significance, where appropriate. d. A secular world view, where appropriate. **All of the above can be taught through the following themes:**
British history	e. Beliefs and concepts: the key ideas and questions of meaning in religions and beliefs, including issues related to God, truth, the world, human life and life after death.
d. The development of political power from the Middle Ages to the twentieth century, including changes in the relationship between rulers and ruled over time, the changing relationship between the crown and parliament, and the development of democracy. e. The different histories and changing relationships through time of the peoples of England, Ireland, Scotland and Wales. f. The impact through time of the movement and settlement of diverse peoples to, from and within the British Isles. g. The way in which the lives, beliefs, ideas and attitudes of people in Britain have changed over time, and the factors – such as technology, economic development, war, religion and culture – that have driven these changes.	f. Authority: different sources of authority and how they inform believers' lives. g. Religion and science: issues of truth, explanation, meaning and purpose. h. Expressing spirituality: how and why understanding of the self and human experiences is expressed in a variety of forms. i. Ethics and relationships: questions and influences that inform ethical and moral choices, including forgiveness and issues of good and evil. j. Rights and responsibilities: what religions and beliefs say about human rights and responsibilities, social justice and citizenship. k. Global issues – what religions and beliefs say about health, wealth, war, animal rights and the environment. l. Interfaith dialogue – a study of relationships, conflicts and collaboration within and between religions and beliefs.

History (cont.)	RE (cont.)
h. The development of trade, colonisation, industrialisation and technology, the British Empire and its impact on different people in Britain and overseas, pre-colonial civilisations, the nature and effects of the slave trade, and resistance and decolonisation. ***European and world history*** i. The impact of significant political, social, cultural, religious, technological and/or economic developments and events on past European and world societies. j. The changing nature of conflict and cooperation between countries and peoples and its lasting impact on national, ethnic, racial, cultural or religious issues, including the nature and impact of the two World Wars and the Holocaust, and the role of European and international institutions in resolving conflicts.	

the interesting possibility of doing studies on contested places, such as the Middle East. This would allow the study of place in terms of its meaning to different people by looking at what is there and why this matters. History could provide the historical context for an understanding of the issues surrounding those who live in the region, whilst the topic opens up possibilities for RE to study different religions and issues of interfaith dialogue and ethics, and citizenship could look at the range of actions that could be taken to resolve tension in the region.

Another example could draw on the citizenship requirement to explore actions of individuals, groups and organisations to influence decisions. The contribution of history to such a theme could involve studying past protest movements as part of an examination of the relationship between rulers and the ruled. In geography the focus could be on interactions between people and their environment, with a focus on environmental groups and their impact. In RE pupils could study the role of beliefs in motivating individuals to stand up and influence decision making, which would also delve into issues about ethics and rights and responsibilities.

In both these examples, the subjects provide different insights into the issue being examined, which collectively should provide pupils with a deeper overall understanding of the issues involved. At the same time though teaching should not simply focus on providing the students with just more information; to do justice fully to the subjects requires the development of conceptual and procedural understanding at the same time, which emphasises the importance of clear and careful planning when approaching any cross-curricular work.

Reflective task 1.2

How might the importance statements help provide a rationale for a cross-curricular approach to humanities teaching?

To what extent do concepts, processes, and range and breadth of content provide a suitable focal point for planning a cross-curricular approach to humanities teaching?

Summary

Reflection on the issues raised in this chapter is an important part of the process of personal development, which is actually central to a sense of professionalism. As teachers we all need to examine our own practice and investigate areas for development and ways to enhance our pedagogical skills and understanding. For those readers undertaking initial teacher education, this would include reflecting on the Q Standards regularly and building an evidence base that demonstrates your effective meeting of them. For those readers already working as teachers, there will be strategies of performance appraisal and review, which involve core (C) standards, and require you to set targets and monitor your process through reflective cycles.

We hope that a suitable target for your own professional development would be to explore how a greater understanding of the other humanities subjects (or indeed any other subject) can enhance your own subject teaching. For example, the following case study illustrates how, at a personal level, an understanding of the humanities subjects can develop.

Case study 1.2: *Richard Harris reflects on his personal understanding*

The way I view the humanities subjects and their value in relation to history and education generally has changed. Reading *The Making of the English Landscape* by W.G. Hoskins was pivotal in helping me to understand the importance of the landscape in history and made me realise the importance of being able to 'read' the landscape. Clearly, powerful geographical forces combined with human interaction shaped the world in which we live, and thus an understanding of the geographical context is a crucial part of creating a deeper historical understanding. My involvement in a number of different educational projects has also reshaped the way I view citizenship. Leading a project on behalf of the Council of Europe called 'Education for the Prevention of Crimes against Humanity' made me rethink my position. Educating *about* crimes against humanity is relatively straightforward from a history perspective but to educate to *prevent* is very different. It has a very distinct educational purpose, firmly grounded in issues of values, morality and action, and although teaching it requires a historical context, to be successful requires an explicit focus in the area of citizenship. Such developments can happen haphazardly, but we hope that this book provides a structured approach to such developments.

To assist with these processes, each chapter in this book, and the accompanying titles within the series, has considered how the text and activities within it have helped the reader meet the Q Standards for Qualified Teacher Status (QTS). A summary of the application of these standards to each chapter appears at the end of each chapter. We trust that you will find this a helpful way of applying your work in reading the chapters (and the completion of any of the activities within them) to your wider professional development.

Professional standards for QTS

This Chapter will help you meet the following Q standards: Q6, Q7a, Q8, Q14, Q15.

Professional standards for teachers

This Chapter will help you meet the following core standards: C6, C7, C8, C15, C16, C40.

2

Cross-curricular approaches to the humanities: how might a school shape its curriculum?

Key objectives

By the end of this chapter, you will have:

■ applied a rationale for a cross-curricular approach to different curriculum models;

■ considered the different ways in which a humanities curriculum can be constructed;

■ analysed the strengths and weaknesses of these different models;

■ drawn on existing literature and case studies to explore models that would work best in your own context.

How schools support a cross-curricular approach to humanities teaching will obviously vary, especially as there are so many different ways that this could be facilitated. For example, where separate subjects are taught, it is obviously much more down to individuals to adopt a cross-curricular perspective, and as such this may be dealt with on an ad hoc basis or by individual arrangements between staff. Even where a school operates a faculty system, approaches to humanities teaching will vary. Many schools still teach identifiable separate subjects within this approach, although within this framework teachers may be expected to teach across all the humanities, either in an integrated approach or teaching distinct subjects, or just within their own specialisms. At one level this can be regarded as an organisational issue, which may or may not support cross-curricular work. Often the choice can be determined by issues that have nothing to do with curriculum rationale, such as budget restrictions, or reorganising timetables to account for part-time teachers or maternity leaves for example. Importantly it is dependent on the attitudes, behaviours and beliefs of teachers to make whatever system is in place work.

The following two case studies provide an insight into different ways a school could approach humanities provision. Neither model is perfect, both are in the early stages of development, but they provide a useful starting point to identify key issues into how to structure a more cross-curricular approach to humanities.

Case study 2.1: *Apple School*

Apple School decided to use the freedom presented by the new National Curriculum to innovate in Year 9 in the latter half of the academic year. The rationale behind this decision was that pupils had made their options choices, and understandably felt they were 'treading water' until their GCSE courses started, and so were quite often disengaged from learning in a number of subject areas, resulting in growing behavioural issues and subsequent frustration on the part of teachers. The curriculum model adopted attempted to address these concerns as well as provide pupils with the necessary transferable skills to enable success at GCSE, a more enjoyable learning experience and a series of topics that were regarded as relevant.

At the heart of the system is the adoption of a thematic curriculum and pupil choice. The curriculum adopted actually brings together the arts (art, drama and music) and humanities (geography, history and RE). Thus the school identified a number of themes, 'Who am I?', 'Where are we going?', 'Money makes the world go round' and 'China, America and Us'. The school decided that there would be a theme per half term, once options had been decided, and all the departments within the arts and humanities areas would provide a 'challenge' for each theme, which gave a subject-specific take on the theme. The choice of content seemed to have been considered seriously, with a keen attempt to study things that students would see as relevant or meaningful.

Students would then do three challenges per theme (out of six offered). The time allocation was substantial. The timetable was written so that four-hour blocks were available. Each challenge would be allocated three blocks of four hours in a two-week period. Therefore each half term, pupils would study one theme, through three subject 'challenges', each of which would be covered in 12 hours. Pupils opted for the challenges they wanted, which were constructed so that pupils had to choose a mix of arts and humanities perspectives. Assessment would focus on transferable skills rather than subject-specific outcomes.

Obviously such a major rethink about the school curriculum needed strong backing from the senior leadership team in the school, which was provided; indeed the senior leadership team were the ones driving the change. The school took the implementation of this model very seriously. Pupils were consulted about the themes they would like to study, a number of which took the staff by surprise, such as 'Money makes the world go round?', which staff felt pupils would find unattractive. There was also a strong evaluation system put in place to monitor the impact of the curriculum changes, and feedback from this process has subsequently led to modifications to the curriculum and the way it is implemented. The staff were also widely consulted about the proposed changes. All the departments were heavily involved in the initial stages in identifying themes, and were given a great deal of freedom in how they would interpret them. Each theme within each subject area would have a major outcome, which would be shared at the end.

When we visited the school, where pupils were starting the theme for that half term, 'China, America and Us', the pupils were engaged in a variety of activities. In history, students were researching major events in the Cold War to examine the relationship between the countries specified in the theme. In geography, students were examining their impressions of China and starting to find out about its culture. In RE, the focus was on religions in China and the United States, with a starting focus on Buddhism. In art, students were re-designing the national flags, using new techniques that they had been taught. In drama, the emphasis was on 'Hollywood history' and how movies 'twist' a story to make it more cinematic. In music, the focus was on developments in American music.

Interviews with the staff involved provided mixed responses about this experiment, although there were a number of things on which all staff expressed similar views. They appreciated the ownership of the process; they had helped to shape the final outcome rather than having it directed. The focus on developing transferable skills was seen as a positive move. The opportunities to bring in local fieldwork and a personal focus within topics, or to study totally different curriculum areas were all seen as benefits. A big bonus was the perceived greater levels of engagement from students; the chance for students to choose topics and the range of creative tasks that were devised were seen as instrumental in providing this, and overall staff felt there had been fewer behavioural issues with students. The staff also felt they taught differently, acting more as facilitators rather than 'teachers', which created a different relationship in the classroom.

Despite these positives a number of staff were divided about the use of a four-hour teaching block; on the one hand it allowed pupils to engage with a topic or task, especially in the practical subjects, but maintaining pace and motivation could be difficult. The staff were also split as to whether they had gained or lost out as a result of the changes. Some were adamant that the 'life skills are more important than knowledge' and so were comfortable with what could be perceived as a loss of normal curriculum time. Others were less happy. In history and to an extent in geography, the staff did not feel the loss of subject-specific teaching time, following the National Curriculum, was compensated by the gains of this curriculum experiment. The focus on transferable skills was at the expense of subject-specific understanding and there were concerns this was not as strong a preparation for GCSE. It was clear that some staff felt, with recent curriculum developments that have been undermining the place of a traditional subject-based curriculum, the adoption of this alternative curriculum within the school was the only way they could preserve the place of their subject.

Talking to pupils also revealed a range of views. The one thing that all the pupils interviewed agreed on was the issue of choice. They really valued the opportunity to have some say in what they wanted to study (although this was only true as long as they were able to get the choices they wanted!). There was however a divergence of views on all other issues, a great deal of which can be explained by the school's policy on setting pupils.

On arrival in Year 7, pupils are set across the school in the majority of subjects. Thus this change in the curriculum, which allowed pupils to choose their challenges, meant that pupils ended up in mixed ability groups. This was seen as a major problem by those pupils who came from the top sets. One pupil had even written a letter, which ran to two sides of A4, to the deputy head, outlining his concerns about the curriculum! These pupils did not like being taught in mixed groups, because, as they rightly pointed out, the teachers were not used to mixed ability classes and so these students felt unchallenged in many of the groups. Although they acknowledged they had opportunities to be more creative in the intended outcomes of the different 'challenges', they felt there was a degree of repetition in the outcomes expected, such as the production of board games. Whereas the teachers had felt the new curriculum had engendered a more positive teacher–student relationship, this group of pupils felt that the constant turnover in groups made it difficult for them to establish a strong group dynamic and that they had little time to build a relationship with the teachers.

The pupils from the middle and lower sets had fewer issues with the new type of groupings, although they felt frustrated by some pupils who were uncooperative in group work situations. Like the more able pupils, they enjoyed the creative side of the challenges and really appreciated those challenges that had associated field trips.

A number of issues emerged from the interviews with pupils. The loudest complaint was about the four-hour blocks. Pace dipped quite considerably in these sessions and the length of time was felt to be inappropriate for many of the challenges (the real benefit was in the practical subjects). The other issue was linked to assessment. Pupils were unclear about what was being assessed and how they were being assessed. Quite often feedback from one challenge did not arrive (if at all) until pupils were deep into their next challenge, and even then pupils were unclear about what they were expected to improve on, or how they were expected to improve. Although there seemed to be a clear rationale for what was studied in terms of content, the students did not necessarily draw on the different perspectives provided by the subject challenges to provide deeper insights into the overall theme.

Case study 2.2: *Pear College*

Unlike Apple School, Pear College has adopted a revised curriculum in Year 7 focused on project-based learning. Again, the range of subjects extended beyond the traditional humanities areas, and included citizenship, PSHE and drama. Each half term is focused on a different project, including 'Different places', 'A sense of place', 'Time team', 'Water world' and 'My island'. Through these projects pupils are expected to develop a range of competences, improve levels of motivation and enhance their literacy skills. In particular the team wanted to focus on ways of presenting, ways of researching, finding and using information, developing teamwork, promoting reflection, evaluation and target setting, and the use of key words. The school had identified these areas, given what they saw as weaknesses pupils had on transfer from Key Stage 2. Once a week, the pupils' normal timetable of five 50-minute lessons would be condensed and they would devote the entire day to their project.

We were able to visit the school and observe the curriculum in action and had opportunities to talk to the staff involved. In terms of planning, the following observations were made and shared with the staff after our visit:

> There is a strong sense that this curriculum is 'owned' by the staff who teach on the programme. They have developed all the materials themselves; they have a clear sense of purpose, which is related to the needs of the pupils within the locality; and they have ensured that the programme is interdisciplinary. The team involved are very enthusiastic about the programme, despite initial reservations, and they have been well supported by the SLT who have encouraged the team to be innovative. The programme is innovative and creative. The team are happy to develop this curriculum as the school operates a traditional three-year KS3, so there is ample opportunity to develop subject-specific expertise in Years 8 and 9. The programme is student centred as it originated from a staff development session about 'what the ideal Pear pupil should be able to do'. The programme is therefore designed to develop generic learning 'skills', so that pupils are better able to access the individual curriculum areas in Years 8 and 9.

Talking to the teachers about the programme showed that they were genuinely enthusiastic about the curriculum. They enjoyed the process of planning and felt the new approach made them teach in different ways that were more creative, focused far more on transferable skills and were less restricted by questions of content coverage. To this end the team took a deliberate decision that anyone could teach any of the units; this would mean the staff would act as facilitators, avoiding a content-led approach; consequently there was less emphasis on subject-specific developments. The teachers also felt that this had benefited their teaching in other year groups, and had actually led to school-wide discussions, not just about what a Pear pupil should be like but what a Pear teacher should be like. For example they talked about developing enquiry-based teaching and learning across the key stage.

The pupils were also enthusiastic about these project-based lessons. In particular they liked the freedom and choice they were given in how to carry out their work, and the practical activities were especially popular. They appreciated the value of working with different members of their peer group and they enjoyed the opportunities for extensive group work. They also liked some of the additional elements which relate more to transition issues, such as the opportunity of being in one place most of the day, not having to move constantly and so forth. The fact that each day had a tangible outcome, usually in some form of presentation, was welcomed.

However, despite these many positives, some concerns were raised. The pupils often felt that the day was too long and they found it hard to stay focused for the whole day. This was a concern also raised by the teaching assistants who supported the programme, as they said that many pupils, especially those with special needs, found the day difficult. The school was also running another project-based learning programme in another area of the school. This was also focused on developing transferable skills, but ironically the pupils were unable to make the connections or demonstrate any cross-over between these two project-based programmes. This suggests that pupils find it just as difficult to transfer learning in a competency-based curriculum from one context to another as they do in a subject-based curriculum. The pupils were not always sure what specific skills they were developing, nor were they sure about how they were supposed to develop these and demonstrate improvement. They did complain that some teachers talked too much, which was little different to what happened in some other lessons!

Reflective task 2.1

Before reading on, consider these case studies and the issues that you are able to identify:

* What seem to be the issues associated with planning and implementing an alternative curriculum?

* What seem to be the issues that need to be considered from the pupils' perspective?

Both case studies provide interesting insights into the challenges of developing any form of cross-curricular model, which are worth considering further. These are explored in more detail below.

Commitment to the development

In both cases support from the senior leadership team was seen as a prerequisite for action; following this the staff were given a large degree of control over the development of the curriculum. Such an approach however means that the staff need to 'buy into' the project and support its rationale, otherwise the potential to subvert what happens is there. In the case of Pear College there did seem to be strong staff 'buy in', with all staff involved talking enthusiastically about the project. At Apple School, although many individual members of staff were committed to the project, this was not universal and some important stakeholders were not fully convinced by the need for the development and/or could not see the benefit of what had been developed. The issue of teacher commitment to change is important. It has long been noted that 'top down' initiatives are more likely to result in failure; for example Williams and Bolem (1993) and Halton (2004) show that a sense of real ownership is crucial. Without this, as van Eekelen, Vermunt and Boshuizen (2006: 408) explain:

> Recent studies concerned with educational innovation have ... shown the majority of such innovations to fail because the teachers – even after a considerable period of time and change – simply abandon the new behaviour and return to comfortable old routines.

However, as Fenwick (2003) has shown this needs to be genuine commitment. Too often, as Fenwick argues, the imposition of a model becomes a self-fulfilling prophecy as individuals are judged against it and in time come to internalise it, even if this model does not quite match the areas for development which teachers feel passionate about. To an extent this can be seen in Apple School, where not all the staff felt the same need to develop this new curriculum model. This is a complex issue to which there is no easy answer, because staff may feel, rightly or wrongly, that what is developed is an inferior 'product' in some ways, depending on what has occurred beforehand. The situation in the school was also complicated by the fact that many teachers felt compelled to adopt this model, as the alternative proposal was to reduce the KS3 curriculum to two years, so these subjects would have lost a considerable amount of curriculum time across the key stage. Some staff therefore felt they were confronted with two unpalatable options, and that what was adopted was the least 'damaging' option for their subject. In such circumstances staff may find it difficult to generate enthusiasm for change and may seek to subvert the rationale behind the new curriculum. This raises important questions about how the school leadership manages such change.

Rationale and coherence of the curriculum

Tyler (1949), in a classic discussion of curriculum development, identified four fundamental questions that are applicable to any curriculum. Essentially the questions are as follows:

- What educational purposes should the school seek to attain?
- What educational experiences can be provided to meet these purposes?

- How can these experiences be organised?
- How can these experiences be assessed to determine whether the purposes have been attained?

The first question is central in developing any rationale for a student's experience of education. Whenever a curriculum is constructed there is a big 'so what' question. Does it matter what pupils learn? The answer should be a resounding yes, but 'the question of knowledge or what it is important that students learn, has been neglected' (Young, 2008: xv). What gets left out is just as important to consider as what gets put in. In a recent critique of curriculum developments, Young (2008) argues persuasively for the centrality of knowledge within the curriculum. This is not merely knowing 'stuff', as that is inert knowledge, but understanding how knowledge is produced in order for students to become critical consumers of knowledge.

In both the cases outlined above, the schools chose a more thematic approach to the curriculum, emphasising a focus on transferable skills or competences to develop pupils' ability to be effective learners. The context for these approaches was rooted in the humanities subjects (and to an extent the arts). The content was therefore based around these subject areas, but ultimately the content mattered less than the skills – but should it be like this? Again this is not an easy question to answer, but it was clear that staff at Pear College had not given this aspect serious consideration. The choice of topics did appear random, which is understandable given the focus on generic skills, as ultimately it could be argued that such skills can be developed regardless of any particular content. At the same time however, more attention could have been given to the selection of content to create a more meaningful experience for the pupils.

At Apple School it was not always clear exactly what each subject was contributing to the overall theme. For example, in the theme 'China, America and us', an art lesson focused on redesigning the flags of these states using different art techniques. The pupils were evidently engrossed in the lesson and there was a lot of productive work, yet what did this lesson do to deepen the pupils' insight into these nations, the interaction between these and the impact and influence of the relationship between these countries? Similarly in music, pupils were learning different songs and tunes from Broadway but it was not clear whether this provided any broader insights for the pupils regarding this theme.

In both schools the pupils did not understand why particular topics were the focus of study. Whilst developing generic skills about learning how to learn are valuable, a focus on these at the expense of subject-specific knowledge is worrying. Students need subject-specific knowledge: not merely content knowledge but a suitably robust understanding of how the subjects work, what distinctive forms of knowledge these subjects produce, how this knowledge emerges and how this helps us to look at the world in different ways. This also requires students to build up a frame of reference, based upon the humanities subjects, into which new knowledge can be placed and contextualised. There is a need for schools to ensure that whatever is taught is coherent.

Changes to teaching and learning or changes to the curriculum

Discussions with staff in both schools raised an issue about what was actually being changed. Were the changes primarily to do with shifting the curriculum focus or a move towards a different teaching and learning approach?

At Apple School, many of the teachers observed in lessons did not seem to have taken the opportunity to pursue new ways of teaching. It seemed the change had been in what was taught, not how it could be taught. Where change was noted, there was a greater emphasis on group work, but this can be a problematic area. At Pear College there was an explicit emphasis on doing things differently; there was an emphasis on enquiry-based learning and promoting creativity, and ensuring there was a sizable outcome to the day's task. A curriculum was devised which staff felt would allow these to be achieved more easily. Yet part of the motivation for doing this was an assumption that this was not possible, given what were perceived as, current curricular constraints. The teachers seemed to feel that following the traditional National Curriculum meant a focus on a content-driven curriculum. This raises the question of whether the staff needed new ways to explore their teaching and learning practice, or whether the real need was to change the curriculum.

Of course it may be possible and desirable to do both. A cross-curricular dimension could be developed, drawing on the distinctive knowledge bases and ways of seeing the world, which enhances pupils' understanding of an issue or theme. And at the same time this could be taught in a more creative, enquiry-orientated fashion.

Developing teaching and learning

Many of the teachers involved in these two schools wished to develop a more investigative approach to learning, using group work more frequently. This was something the pupils endorsed, saying they enjoyed group work, but only when the group was able to work effectively together. This suggests teachers need to pay more attention to developing effective pupil–pupil talk. Yet the research evidence shows that many teachers fail to capitalise on pupil talk. In particular two issues emerge.

Kutnick et al.'s (2005) review of the literature on pupil grouping shows that teachers tend to place pupils in groups, within class, for organisational or behavioural reasons, rather than matching the type of task being tackled to the group composition. They identify different types of task and match these to different sizes of groups (see Tables 2.1 and 2.2 overleaf)

Imagine for example a series of lessons on ways in which a society can tackle poverty. The topics can easily draw upon all the humanities subjects. In terms of citizenship, pupils can explore the options which face government organisations and charities when trying to tackle poverty, and explore the pros and cons of current policies. History can provide a contextual background by looking at past attempts to deal with poverty, such as the Elizabethan Poor Laws and the development of poor relief from the eighteenth century through to the setting up of the Welfare State. Geography can provide an alternative context by looking at patterns of wealth around the globe and exploring why some countries are wealthier than others, but also explore how some countries are now moving into a period of rapid economic expansion and the problems this creates. RE

Table 2.1 Group size and match to learning task

Group size	Learning task
Individual	Practice Revision
Dyad	Incremental Restructuring
Triad	Incremental Restructuring with computer or other apparatus
Small group	Enrichment Restructuring
Large group	Incremental
Whole class	Incremental Practice Revision

Table 2.2 Different types of learning task

Definitions of classroom learning tasks (from Norman, 1978)
Incremental: Introduces new ideas, procedures or skills, or demands recognition or discrimination (also referred to as a cognitive task)
Restructuring: Demanding a child invents or discovers an idea for him/herself (a cognitive task)
Enrichment: Demands application or synthesis of familiar skills to a new problem (an application task)
Practice: Demands the tuning of new skills on familiar problems
Revision: Demands the use of skills that have not been used for some time

may focus on the work of charitable organisations, but may equally look at the beliefs of different faiths towards helping others, and therefore explore attitudes towards helping those in difficulty.

Within these lessons, pupils are given different case studies to consider, which cover issues of poverty within the UK and abroad. Pupils explore the role that charitable organisations and the government play in tackling poverty. The teacher starts off with a whole-class discussion to identify pupils' existing knowledge; where gaps in their knowledge exist or misconceptions are identified the teacher provides some verbal explanation to elaborate and clarify pupils' understanding. The pupils then work individually, using textbooks and worksheets to find out information about the role of different charities and their attempts to tackle poverty. The teacher then provides an explanation to the whole class about the way the government addresses this issue at home and abroad, and the students are invited to discuss as a class whether the government could or should play a larger role in tackling poverty at home and abroad.

Now if we analyse what the pupils are doing, what they are expected to be able to do and the ways in which the teacher gets pupils to work, we can start to explain whether this approach is suitable.

At the start the teacher is trying to identify pupils' starting points, which is good practice; once it is clear that pupils need more specific information to build their knowledge base or to address misconceptions, we can see that the pupils are engaged in an 'incremental' task. This can be done as a whole class, but could equally be done by getting pupils to work in twos or threes. The second part of the lesson, where pupils work individually, is also an 'incremental' task and so the use of individual work is less effective here. The teacher input on the role of government is also an 'incremental' task, so a whole-class approach can be effective, but the follow-up discussion is an 'enrichment' task where pupils are being asked to synthesise their new-found knowledge to argue a particular case; this is better done in small groups rather than as a whole class.

Practical task 2.1

Identify a lesson you have taught recently and look closely at the specific activities you asked pupils to do. Try to decide what type of learning activity these were according to the definitions above.

Now look at the way you organised the class for these activities and decide whether your choice of grouping was appropriate for the activity. How well were the learning activities and groupings matched.

Plan a new lesson taking into account the type of learning activities and most effective groupings. Having taught the lesson reflect on the impact that matching activity to grouping had to the success to the lesson.

Another issue identified in the research literature is that few teachers give enough explicit attention to developing pupils' ability to work effectively within groups, which is often dependent on the ability of pupils to communicate effectively as a group. Edwards and Mercer (1987) and Mercer (1995, 2000) argue that most talk in the classroom is teacher talk, and most of that is instructional; pupil talk on the other hand is neglected. Where pupil talk occurs, it is not always productive. Mercer (1995) categorises three different types of children's talk in collaborative groups: disputational, cumulative and exploratory. Disputational talk is essentially an exchange of opposite views marked by disagreement. In the cumulative situation pupils build uncritically on what others have said. In the exploratory situation pupils engage critically with each other and help to construct new understandings. Exploratory talk is the ideal and holds out the possibility of enabling an informed exchange of ideas, which would be highly desirable when addressing controversial issues, but it seems infrequently used or developed (see Chapter 5 for a further discussion). This was witnessed this during a cross-curricular project where humanities teachers and science teachers came together to focus on controversial socio-scientific issues (Harris and Ratcliffe, 2005). One of the main problems noted was the lack of suitable discussion skills amongst students. Where exploratory talk was observed, the quality of discussion was considerably higher, but this was the exception rather than the rule (it was actually only observed in one school out of the eight schools involved in the project). In most cases teachers had to lead the discussions from the front; pupil input and interactions between pupils were limited and so it was difficult to judge the extent to which pupils had grasped key ideas or had been forced to explore alternative positions. It would seem therefore that teachers need further support in moving towards an enquiry-based approach to learning. By developing teachers' pedagogical ability to instigate and manage discussion, the role of the teacher would change from being centre stage to being a facilitator and this would in turn promote pupil independence and higher-level thinking.

Transferability and assessment issues

The focus on developing generic competences poses particular difficulties. A criticism of the traditional subject-based curriculum is that pupils adopt a 'silo' approach to thinking, and only apply particular ideas and ways of thinking when taught within a particular subject. For example, ideas about how to write effectively may be taught within English or history, yet few pupils will take the principles gained and apply them in other settings. The recent emphasis on 'Personal, Learning and Thinking Skills' is part of an attempt to overcome this problem, but a cross-curricular approach to learning is also seen as a way of developing the ability to apply new skills across learning experiences. However interviews with pupils at Pear College suggest this is still a problem even within a strong cross-curricular environment. The school has already developed a unit on project-based learning in another area of the school curriculum, and although the humanities-based component was based on a similar approach and set of principles, the pupils did not make the connection. Instead the pupils saw the two approaches as separate 'subjects', so to speak, and therefore the potential of building upon transferable skills was not being fully exploited.

The second issue is associated with assessment. Trying to identify progression within a subject is hard enough at times, but trying to identify progression regarding generic skills is a very challenging task. Yet it is crucial if we want pupils to develop these abilities and to be able to set sensible targets.

For example, if we take the area of developing enquiry skills, we can break this down into different areas: asking questions/identifying issues, action planning, seeking and using resources, organising and communicating information, and evaluating what has been done and setting targets. Within each of these strands, pupils could move from little independence, where the teacher makes all the decisions or provides all the resources and feedback, to a point where pupils are completely autonomous. For this to be successful, teachers need to unpick this very carefully, and plan how and where pupils will develop these skills.

Both case study schools had adopted booklets to support the assessment of the skills identified, where students received feedback and had the opportunity to engage in target setting. Apple School realised that this system was not working efficiently so was going to rethink its approach. The teachers at Pear College thought the booklets were working well, having gained some feedback from parents and pupils, but interviews with the pupils showed they had little real understanding of what they were being assessed against, nor how they were supposed to get better at these skills in the future.

The challenges associated with assessment within the humanities are explored in greater depth in Chapter 7 of this book.

Time

The two case studies also raise the interesting question of how much time needs to be given to different curriculum models. Both schools invest a great deal of time, in large blocks, to facilitate students' learning. At one level this is appreciated by students, who feel they can 'get to grips' with a topic and have the time to see something through to completion without having to break away from it. This is particularly true where any practical work is involved. However pupils in both schools highlighted the difficulties of maintaining concentration and interest for such long periods and, despite the best efforts of teachers, the pace of the sessions did flag considerably. The result was often a last-minute rush to finish things or a tailing off of interest. Again there seem to be no specific rules governing what is the optimum time allocation which should be given to cross-curricular work, but it is something that needs to be considered in any planning.

> ## Reflective task 2.2
>
> Having read the previous section:
> * What seem to be the big issues facing you and/or your school in developing a cross-curricular approach to humanities teaching?
> * What lessons can you learn from the experiences outlined in these case studies? What other issues might you have to consider in your context?

Concluding thoughts

There are obviously a number of different ways a school, faculty, department or individual could create a cross-curricular approach to humanities. To an extent this is an organisational issue, which may or may not facilitate more effective models of cross-curricular learning. An approach which promotes separate subjects or allows staff to teach within their specialisms is more likely to depend on the disposition of individuals to pursue an integrated approach to the humanities. This is not to denigrate such a model, as excellent subject teaching is obviously essential and may well be more beneficial than having a cross-curricular model that inadequately develops pupils' understanding of the subjects. But an integrated approach obviously requires teachers to understand the nature of the range of subjects and what they offer. Or, if the focus is on generic competences, the staff need to give serious consideration to issues of progression, assessment and content selection. Any form of integrated approach, in order to be successful, needs the support and understanding of the staff involved. None of which is easy!

Clearly the models presented above are those that have been constructed at a whole-school level and require thinking and planning across a number of staff, yet there is much that you can do as an individual in your own classroom to promote a more integrated approach to humanities. As an individual, it is important that you have considered the materials presented in Chapter 1 of this book, where the nature and purpose of the different humanities subjects are discussed, as this is the first step in considering a cross-curricular approach. The remaining chapters, though, will give you the opportunity to consider pedagogical approaches which can be used by any individual as a means of promoting a more effective cross-curricular approach.

Professional standards for QTS

This chapter will help you meet the following Q standards: Q6, Q7a, Q8, Q18, Q33.

Professional standards for teachers

This chapter will help you meet the following core standards: C6, C7, C8, C15, C18, C35, C40.

3

Approaches to teaching and learning in the humanities and beyond

Key objectives

By the end of this chapter, you will have:

■ reflected upon what you think constitutes good teaching and learning in general;

■ considered what constitutes good teaching and learning in the humanities subjects;

■ evaluated different approaches to teaching cross-curricular work in two humanities subjects;

■ considered some key principles that can be used in planning and teaching cross-curricular humanities work;

■ identified potential areas for cross-curricular work in and beyond the humanities subjects.

Before we can explore what effective approaches to teaching cross-curricular humanities are, first let us consider, in general, what are effective approaches to teaching and learning? The answer is arguably pretty clear. It is all in a word.

Teachers do not just want to be '*satisfactory*', they want to be seen as '*good*'. Better still if they can achieve the holy grail of being '*outstanding*'; then everyone is happy. Of course we are talking about Ofsted grading here. We would all be lying to ourselves if we didn't want to be seen as good teachers who teach our subjects well. If you have ever been through an Ofsted inspection, and if you are lucky or unlucky enough to be observed, one of the things your colleagues want to know is what grade or word you were given. In fact in most cases SLTs use the same framework as Ofsted when observing lessons for performance management purposes. They should therefore know what they are looking for. So, what does make a good or an outstanding lesson?

Practical task 3.1

You need to work with another colleague on this task.

1. On your own come up with two lists. One list should describe what you think constitutes outstanding teaching; the second should describe outstanding learning.

2. Now share your set of criteria with your colleague. Do you have the same items?

3. Between you try to come up with a definitive list.

We hope that you found practical task 3.1 quite tricky. After all what does constitute 'outstanding' teaching and learning? Can it be boiled down to a checklist? Many schools have created such lists to use in lesson observations. One problem with this approach has been that until very recently Ofsted have kept what they are looking for a secret. A few years ago one of the authors of this book was asked to run some INSET on 'outstanding teaching' for a group of history teachers. After he'd sat down to plan the session, it soon became apparent that it was difficult to define what 'outstanding' looked like. Maybe Ofsted documentation would be a help? But where was the Ofsted framework? What were the criteria they used to judge lessons? This couldn't be easily located on the Ofsted website. Did the head teacher know? When asked, he simply scratched his head, then looked in his filing cabinets and searched on the internet but he too could not find the sacred document. Eventually we stumbled across it (and the head quickly filed it away). How useful was this piece of paper? Did it help work out what constitutes an outstanding lesson? This is what the September 2005–2009 Ofsted criteria said for outstanding:

> Outstanding (1) – The lesson is at least good in all major respects and is exemplary in significant elements as shown by the significant progress made by all of the learners.

This is at best vague. Maybe that was the intention? It does not tell us anything helpful. The key words are probably 'significant progress made by all of the learners'. But even this is hard to measure in a classroom. You may have heard of stories where, when asked what makes a lesson outstanding, inspectors reply by saying, 'you'll know when you see it.' Or, it has 'the wow factor'. All of this is very unhelpful, especially if your performance is being judged termly by senior leaders who have to interpret what this one sentence means in a classroom setting. However, from September 2009 clearer guidance was on its way – or was it? Ofsted introduced their latest framework. This gave more detail about what constitutes 'outstanding' teaching. It also formally introduced the notion of how teachers use assessment (Ofsted, 2009b: 31).

Practical task 3.2

Do your lists from practical task 3.1 agree with any of the points made in the Ofsted framework below?

Outstanding (1) – Teaching is at least good and much is outstanding, with the result that the pupils are making exceptional progress. It is highly effective in inspiring pupils and ensuring that they learn extremely well. Excellent subject knowledge is applied consistently to challenge and inspire pupils. Resources, including new technology, make a marked contribution to the quality of learning, as does the precisely targeted support provided by other adults. Teachers and other adults are acutely aware of their pupils' capabilities and of their prior learning and understanding, and plan very effectively to build on these. Marking and dialogue between teachers, other adults and pupils are consistently of a very high quality. Pupils understand in detail how to improve their work and are consistently supported in doing so. Teachers systematically and effectively check pupils' understanding throughout lessons, anticipating where they may need to intervene and doing so with striking impact on the quality of learning.

Is this any more helpful? It clearly gives some key points. Again it talks about progress – this time students need to make 'exceptional progress'. It also states that teaching should 'inspire' pupils and help them 'learn extremely well'. What this actually looks like though is still difficult to define. Also, roughly half of the statement refers to the use of assessment. This is in principal to be lauded. After all, if teachers do not know exactly where their students are at then they simply cannot pitch the lesson so it meets their needs. Marking and dialogue between teachers and pupils should be of a high quality because this will help pupils understand how to improve their work. This is in theory a very good benchmark. However, in practice this obsession with assessment is dangerous. Not when used by Ofsted inspectors necessarily, but when used and interpreted by school leaders who sometimes think this means that students should know what National Curriculum level they are at. This can make teachers think that outstanding teaching is about levelling pieces of work and students knowing how to achieve the next level. Fine in theory but in practice it is not that simple. This is a blind alley, as we discuss in Chapter 7. Also, outstanding teaching must be more than levels and marking. It must have something to do with activities planned by the teacher. Ofsted are due to publish yet another framework for inspections in 2012. Maybe this will be more accommodating?

Where else do we look if we want to know what constitutes effective teaching in the humanities subjects? In recent Ofsted subject-specific reports (2010a and b, 2011a and b) inspectors have listed, from their observations, suggestions of what makes effective teaching in the humanities subjects. This has been summarised in Table 3.1 below.

Table 3.1 *Characteristics of effective teaching in the humanities subjects according to Ofsted*

Citizenship	Geography
■ Teachers showed their good or outstanding subject knowledge in a range of ways. ■ Good teachers of Citizenship recognised the importance of topicality to develop students' knowledge and understanding. ■ The better Citizenship teachers ensured that students gained the knowledge they needed in order to have something worthwhile to say. ■ Managing discussion of sensitive and controversial issues can be very demanding, but confident teachers made such lessons worthwhile. ■ The most effective lessons seen often used high-quality resources very well. ■ ICT provides good opportunities for Citizenship teaching and for learning through enquiry.	■ Teachers' high expectations ensured positive responses from students; for example, when they expected well-informed answers to their questions they received them. ■ Work was interesting and dealt with contemporary issues and developments; teachers stayed up to date and incorporated news broadcasts and articles from newspapers or journals into lessons. ■ The clear structure of lessons and the reinforcement of learning objectives meant that it was clear what was expected and how the task should be approached. ■ There was an intensity in the pace of learning in the lessons with no slack time. ■ Compiling helpful revision notes was a continuing part of the course. Revision booklets and revision support groups ensured that all students entered examinations confident that they could succeed. ■ In examination classes, lessons went beyond the basic requirements of the syllabus, with ideas that developed thinking, demonstrated outcomes and enriched the students' geographical vocabulary. ■ Each unit of work identified opportunities for students to consolidate and enhance cross-curricular skills such as literacy, numeracy, ICT and practical Citizenship. ■ The teaching enabled students to develop moral and cultural awareness, for example by exploring topics such as immigration, asylum and refugees, international aid and trade issues, climate change and human rights. ■ Teachers built in opportunities for students to develop enterprise, financial skills and teamwork, both in lessons and during fieldwork.

Citizenship (cont.)	Geography (cont.)
	■ Students were encouraged to develop social skills through participating in Geography fieldwork and, in particular, during residential trips where they were working and living together in unfamiliar environments. ■ Well-taught topics such as 'Population' in Year 8 and 'Climate change' in Year 9 enabled students to develop an understanding of their global responsibilities in relation to human rights and the environment.
History	**RE**
■ Teachers' excellent subject knowledge, clear exposition and judicious selection of teaching strategies, including the use of ICT. ■ A high level of challenge which obliged students to make well-considered judgements based on evidence that was robust and increasingly broad in its range. ■ High-quality activities: students were engaged in presenting and developing ideas, arguing about the past and re-evaluating their thinking in the light of what they had been learning. ■ Sufficient opportunities for students to listen, discuss and debate questions and to respond thoughtfully so that others could comment. ■ The development of historical thinking, analysis and evaluation at the heart of the lesson rather than as an afterthought at the end. ■ A climate of historical enquiry in which trying to find the right answer really mattered to the students and where they developed an understanding of the complexities of the past. ■ Out-of-classroom activities, available for all students, which enriched learning. ■ Careful monitoring of progress by teachers during lessons and regular assessment, including peer- and self-assessment, which enabled students to know how well they were doing and what they had to do to improve.	■ Strong subject expertise. ■ Challenging activities designed to develop higher-order thinking skills. ■ Careful matching of tasks to students' differing needs and abilities. ■ Specific strategies to tackle underachievement of specific groups such as boys. ■ Effective use of a good range of resources, including electronic media. ■ Well-structured discussion and investigative work to promote learning. ■ Regular visits and visitors to enrich learning. ■ Carefully planned activities that promoted collaborative learning through problem solving and discussion. ■ A consistent focus on enabling students to express their personal beliefs, feelings and fears without danger of ridicule or criticism. ■ Careful use of data to analyse students' performance, to set clear and challenging targets and to monitor progress. ■ Effective arrangements for assessing students' progress through peer and self-assessment, and plenary sessions ■ High-quality marking that helped students to identify how they were progressing and precisely what they needed to do to improve their work.

There are some common elements that appear here. The reports for citizenship, history and RE clearly state that excellent or good subject knowledge or expertise are characteristics seen in effective classrooms. Another common feature is that effective classrooms have high levels of challenge. This was mentioned in the geography, history and RE reports. A third element that appears in three of the four lists was that of classroom talk, discussion and debate. The final common attribute seen in three of the four lists was that of pupils learning through problem solving or enquiry – again this was only missing in the geography section. Other common elements that appear in at least two subjects were the use of high-quality resources, teaching focusing on topical events, enrichment activities and the careful monitoring of pupil progress.

Hann (2010) offers some more generic advice on what constitutes outstanding teaching and learning. He draws on the Ofsted framework as well as the key principles of Assessment for Learning (AfL), Personal Learning and Thinking Skills (PLTS), and Social and Emotional Aspects of Learning (SEAL) to come up with the descriptions in Table 3.2.

Table 3.2 'Characteristics of outstanding teaching and learning' according to Hann, from 'You've Been Framed' (2010), adapted from *The Leader Magazine* (ASCL)

Outstanding Teaching	Outstanding Learning
Teacher conveys enthusiasm, enjoyment, confidence and a 'can do' attitude.	Students are excited and enthusiastic. They feel safe, motivated and confident. They tackle learning without fear of failure.
Rapport with students is inspirational. The teacher knows what excites, intrigues and motivates his or her students.	Students know their target and what to do in order to improve their learning. In achieving this, they show resilience and responsibility.
Periods of teacher led information transfer are short, innovative and lead to a desire to know more.	Students engage fully and make progress through sensitive and insightful questioning.
Student activity dominates the lesson. It is differentiated and promotes further exploration.	Students investigate independently, leading each other through their learning.
Review sessions are frequent, student led and lead to application of learning in the lesson as well as potentially in other areas.	Students fully engage with review periods. They give appropriate feedback to the teacher and each other, confirming outstanding learning.

Many points made by Hann here are important elements that can help us understand what effective teaching and learning are. However, some points are open to interpretation. After all what does 'students investigate independently, leading each other through their learning' really mean? Some may think that, for a lesson to be judged as outstanding, for long periods of time pupils will be working alone or collaboratively at an independent level. In reality, many of us who have taught in mixed ability classrooms will know that this is a wonderful yet sometimes seemingly unachievable aim if, as Ofsted stipulate, *all* learners need to make *exceptional* progress. We must remember the limitations of such lists. After all, investigating independently can mean working for 30 seconds or two minutes. We need to be clear that the challenge is pitched to the needs of the individual pupil. Using the above list one may think that if students are engaged in activities then the lesson is more likely to be outstanding. It surely depends on the activities that the teacher has set up, and how the activities link together to help develop pupil understanding.

Thompson (2009) also provides his criteria for what he thinks outstanding means in the history classroom. Many of his points are the same as, or similar to, those given in recent Ofsted reports. Only one of the 12 points refers to history, the rest are generic, and to our minds give clearer guidance about what to look out for in an outstanding lesson:

1. Teacher has a very secure subject knowledge, which is used to enthuse pupils, not just to inform, them. The teacher knows the detail which will fascinate pupils and illuminate key points.

2. An air of excitement often pervades the room because the approaches chosen are interesting, original, innovative or even risky. Pupils are often engrossed, with all feeling involved and the reluctant sensitively coaxed.

3. Teacher sets work which is genuinely challenging and makes pupils feel they have worked hard to grasp a new idea or concept – what HMI have called 'satisfyingly difficult'.

4. Teacher knows how to engage and motivate from the start of a lesson, linking to pupils' prior experience and interests. Teacher connects the topic to first-hand evidence around them, making good use of local examples, and to news items. Teacher knows how to stimulate pupils' curiosity. Pupils actually ask as well as answer questions .This is fairly routine.

5. Teacher confidently designs activities which enable pupils to genuinely work as historians. Teacher knows effective ways of helping pupils to improve their conceptual understanding, for example building up a mental map of the past through clever use of timelines, often on display on walls or IWB. Teacher strikes right balance between informative exposition and encouraging pupils to enquire for themselves.

6. Teacher ensures pupils work at the optimum pace, deliberately injecting new information to build urgency. Mini-plenaries during the lesson enable teacher to check pupils' understanding.

7. Teacher makes sure that pupils work productively in pairs/groups, deliberately varying the grouping to match the intended outcomes. Pupils are competent at evaluating each others' work and know what they need to do in order to improve.

8. Teacher knows exactly how to develop pupils' understanding through careful and progressive questioning, which is usually open, encouraging, well pitched and well directed. Teacher knows how to encourage lively, focused discussion and shows real interest in pupils' ideas, even their misconceptions are skilfully worked on.

9.   Teacher knows how to improve the quality of pupils' written answers. Teacher models good use of language showing degrees of certainty and helps pupils to show respect for evidence. Teacher provides opportunities for pupils to present their findings orally, in writing and through ICT, making sure the imaginative outcomes are modelled for quality.

10.   Teacher offers pupils a rich variety of source material in different formats, including multimedia. Teacher shows imagination in selecting resources and using them in interesting ways, including enabling students to access them independently.

11.   Teacher encourages pupils to reach independent conclusions, substantiating what they say with carefully selected evidence.

12.   Teacher is confident, sensitive and objective in handling controversial moral and political issues and does not fight shy of them.

All of this appears to be good advice. Although some points made by Ofsted in the subject-specific reports and by Thompson relate to one subject, many points are generic and can be applied to teaching and learning in cross-curricular humanities.

Practical task 3.3

Look back at the lists you made in practical task 3.1. Do you need to change this in the light of what you have just read? Come up with a list of between eight and ten points to show what you think you should see in an outstanding cross-curricular humanities lesson.

What constitutes effective teaching and learning in cross-curricular humanities?

How should we approach teaching in cross-curricular humanities? We argue in Chapter 1 that it is possible to look at the concepts of different subjects as described in the 2008 National Curriculum and see where they overlap. This can then be used as a planning tool to knit together units of work. Alternatively, specific content can be used as the vehicle to drive the cross-curricular work. But what do we need to bear in mind when trying to plan for meaningful and rigorous cross-curricular work?

Practical task 3.4

You are going to review a lesson which has combined geography and history in a competency-style curriculum. The teacher is not a specialist in either subject. The unit of work was designed to help the pupils develop their understanding of the locality they live in and develop their generic skills or competences. As the school delivers the humanities subjects through a competency-style curriculum this was also an ideal opportunity to develop the pupils' conceptual understanding of geography and history, and potentially of citizenship.

* What concepts from the subjects would you expect to see developed? Chapter 1 had some suggestions here.

* What points from your criteria for effective teaching would you hope to see in the lesson?

Read through case study 3.1 below. Does the teacher develop the same concepts that you predicted? What elements of effective teaching can you spot? What advice would you give the teacher to help her develop even further?

Case study 3.1: *Designing and evaluating a locality-based monopoly board game*

This was the last of a series of 12 one-hour lessons. The teacher wanted the Year 7 pupils to develop their skills of teamwork, negotiation, communication, cooperation and delegation. She also wanted the pupils to develop their understanding of the locality in which they lived. At the beginning of the lesson the teacher praised the pupils' efforts over the last half term. They had, in groups of four, all produced their own local monopoly-style games – one game per group.

All of the colourful boards were handed out. The teacher recapped the skills the class had developed over the last six weeks by asking closed questions. Individuals answered with words such as teamwork and negotiation. The teacher also stressed to the class that they had learnt about the geography of their local area. The rest of the lesson was simple. In groups of four the students were going to play their games. After that they were going to evaluate them.

The pupils were well behaved and enjoyed the fruits of their labour. In discussions with each group, it became clear that they had had to work together to create and develop their games. Some groups did this very well and democratically. Inevitably some did not and individuals felt that some members had not pulled their weight.

When asked questions about the subject-specific knowledge and skills that had been developed about the locality, the students' answers were vaguer. They had not been out to visit the local area to research their game. They had not considered the pricing of houses or streets when they decided where to put the streets on the board. When they were designing the 'Community Chest' and 'Chance' cards, the teacher had not encouraged them to make cards which would give the players new knowledge of the locality in which they lived or the rich history of the local area. One card read, 'Your dog bit someone – pay a fine of ten pounds.'

The students clearly enjoyed playing the games. After they had finished it was time for the class to review and evaluate them. The teacher asked the class to decide on the criteria that could be used to judge whether the games were good. She wrote the agreed criteria on the board. They included points such as 'fun to play' and 'colourfully designed'. However, the teacher did not encourage the class to think about criteria linked to geographical or historical skills or knowledge. This was surprising as the scheme of work was designed around a theme that related learning to a local context.

Clearly this lesson had some positive elements to it. The teacher had used her generic teaching skills to check learning through question-and-answer sessions. She must also have modelled what a good board game looked like so that the class could see what they were aiming for. The pupils' behaviour was good and they enjoyed evaluating the games. Arguably they developed some of the competences the teacher had wanted them to, such as teamworking and cooperation. But as an example of cross-curricular humanities work, the lesson and the entire scheme of work are clearly lacking. The teachers involved in planning this unit had not really given any thought to the subject-specific concepts or knowledge that the pupils needed to develop.

This was an ideal opportunity to use the content of the locality to develop the class's conceptual understanding of humanities subjects. For geography this would have been a perfect way to develop the children's conceptual understanding of place and space. The teachers could have used the locality and the game to help the class develop their understanding of where this place is. They could have used maps and aerial photographs to help them. Also, they could have thought about questions such as 'What is this place like?' and 'Why is this place like it is?' The children could then have thought about the buildings and their functions, the shops and where they were located, the people and the type of work they did and the houses that they lived in. This would have armed the class with knowledge to design their boards more effectively and helped them with ideas for the creation of their Community Chest-style cards. To link the geography more closely to history, the focus could have been shifted to 'How has this place changed?' and 'How is it changing?' This would have helped develop the notion of change and continuity. They could then have thought about change over time and looked for evidence of this change in buildings, street maps and landscape. If the game was aimed at developing the class's understanding of geography, history and citizenship, then the focus could have been shifted to thinking more about the identity and diversity of the people living in the local area.

All of these opportunities were lost; probably because the teachers who designed this scheme of work did not understand the concepts which underpin geography, history and citizenship. Indeed in our discussions with the teacher she could not identify one organising concept for history or geography. In any case the focus seems to have been more about developing the generic competences of teamwork and cooperation.

This is fine as a by-product of learning in humanities, but it is worrying when these competences become the main focus of the learning of a six-week unit of work. After all, this particular competency-based curriculum replaced the teaching of the traditional humanities subjects in the school. The primary purpose of this six-week unit on 'our locality' surely should be to learn some geography/history/citizenship/RE *and* to develop the said competences. In this particular example, if no real geography or history is learnt in this unit, where else will it be learnt? It is the opinion of the authors of this book that the humane subjects are too important to be neglected in this way. Children can and should learn teamwork, collaboration and cooperation in all lessons. But if competences such as teamwork and cooperation replace the teaching of the humane subjects, or any subject for that matter, then such an approach surely must be questioned.

Practical task 3.5

You are going to review a different lesson which has combined geography and history. This time the teacher is a history subject specialist. In our discussions with him he told us that he had worked very closely with a geography colleague to plan and resource the scheme of work, which was taught as part of a creativity project to Year 7 in a two-week enrichment programme. Six humanities teachers delivered this two-week programme to all of Year 7. Again the unit of work was designed to help the pupils develop their understanding of the locality they live in.

* What concepts from the subjects would you expect to see developed? Chapter 1 had some suggestions here.

* What points from your criteria for effective teaching would you hope to see in the lesson?

Read through case study 3.2 below. Does the teacher develop the same concepts that you predicted? What elements of effective teaching can you spot? What advice would you give the teacher to help him develop even further?

Case study 3.2: *The shabbiest street in Britain?*

This was the first session of a two-week enrichment programme. The lesson started with the teacher showing the class a series of photographs. Could they work out what they were showing and where they were? After the second image it became clear to the children that the photographs were all taken in their local area.

They all easily identified the local leisure centre, the theatre and the library. All hands shot up when the next image was projected. The teacher then asked them to see if they could locate the images on a map of the local area? He was checking to see how much they understood about their locality and their sense of place. Clearly the students knew their stuff as they confidently pinpointed the locations of all five photographs. Next, the teacher introduced an aerial photograph of another location in the local area. Could the class work out where it was? The photo depicted a concrete car park and street located next to Worthing train station. The car park was situated on the site of a 1960s style shopping precinct that thirty years before had been the height of modern architecture. By the mid 1990s it had begun to appear dilapidated, and was then demolished. Nothing replaced it. The class immediately recognised the place as Teville Gate, and again confidently located the car park and street on the map.

The teacher then handed out a newspaper report. The headline read: 'Is this the shabbiest street in Britain?' The class read through the first two paragraphs and realised that the report was describing their local car park and street. At this point the teacher introduced the enquiry question – 'Has Teville Gate always been the shabbiest street in Britain?' The challenge had been set. But how would the class go about finding out? The teacher asked what evidence they would need to work out the answer. Pairs discussed this for a couple of minutes and then fed back ideas such as asking people, looking at maps, reading newspaper reports and going to the library to find local history books.

The teacher then started to distribute a series of maps of the Teville Gate area. Pupils worked in pairs and threes. The first was from 2010. After the class gained their bearings with the map – they located the train station, the car park and Teville Road – the teacher introduced a second map, this time from 1970. They were asked to identify anything that had changed between 1970 and 2010. Little had changed; they could see that the train station and the car park were still there, but the precinct that had recently been knocked down had been standing in 1970. A further map was then distributed, this time from 1952. At this point the class noticed a number of important changes. The car park and the shopping precinct had vanished. Instead it seemed that houses with gardens stood where the car park now was and the precinct had been. This was a dramatic change.

The teacher asked if we could tell what the houses were like from the map. Some of them were clearly bigger than the others and had longer gardens; some were connected together in a terrace. The teacher then introduced a map from 1910 which still displayed the same houses, but this time a stream appeared at the end of some of the gardens. A map from 1870 again clearly showed the same houses. A final map from 1848 was introduced. This time there were no houses, just fields. The only similarity to today was the existence of the train station.

At this point the class were encouraged to come up with their own questions – What were the houses from the nineteenth century actually like? Why had they been knocked down? Who lived in them? What were these people like? The teacher wrote the questions on the board and explained that, if they could find out the answer to these questions they could work out the answer to the big enquiry question: had Teville Gate always been the shabbiest street in Britain? Clearly the maps showed how the area had changed over time, and the children had realised that the two biggest changes had happened between 1840 and 1870 and then between1952 and 1970. But they needed more evidence to really get a sense of place and understand change in a deeper sense.

At this point the teacher introduced a photograph of the street dating from 1900. There was a horse and cart and a row of chimneys, but the style and size of the houses were obscured by an avenue of trees. Although the houses looked as if they might be large, using the photograph one simply couldn't tell exactly what they were like. The class were asked how else they could find out. He listened attentively to answers before introducing some new evidence – a part of the 1891 census for the Teville Gate area. Each pupil was given a character who appeared in the census and lived in a house in the street. They were given the person's name and address, their age, their marital status and their job. The class were asked to walk around and mix with each other to find the other people who lived with them in the same house. They really enjoyed doing this. After about five minutes they had found their families, lodgers and servants. They were then told that they were at a street party and that they should meet their neighbours. They went around introducing themselves to each other.

The teacher then asked them to create a continuum of social standing – with the most important person at one end and the least important at the other. The class did this well. Each person in the line described who they were and why they were standing where they were. Through this process it became clear that the people who lived in the street were quite wealthy, some had servants, and others had retired and lived off 'their own means'. The teacher then reminded the class of the enquiry question: Had Teville Gate always been the shabbiest street in Britain? The pupils now had enough evidence to make a more informed judgement. They said that it hadn't been that shabby in 1890 because the census suggested otherwise and this agreed with what they thought the photographs had shown. Their inference was that some of the houses were large – because, using the census material, the people who lived in them appeared to be wealthy.

The scheme of work then allowed the children to go for a walk and visit the Teville Gate area; it also helped the class understand how and why the houses had been knocked down, and they came up with their own regeneration scheme for the area which they designed and presented to local businessmen and members of the council.

This example of cross-curricular work took the same starting point as case study 3.1 – to make content-based links. In this case the content was the local area. Also, like case study 3.1 it started small and tried to link just two subjects. But it differs in many ways.

Case study 3.2 is very good example of what effective teaching and learning in cross-curricular humanities might look like. Nine principles shine through the planning and teaching of this cross-curricular project which are worth thinking about if and when teachers want to create effective chunks of cross-curricular humanities work:

1. This project aimed at making content based links.

2. The unit of work was planned by a subject specialist who really understood his subject – history.

3. He also sought advice from and collaborated in planning the unit with a colleague who was a geography expert and really understood what good geography is.

4. It was clear that the teachers involved in this project had thought through exactly what it was that they wanted to achieve. They clearly wanted to develop their pupils' understanding of the locality in which they lived, and wanted the pupils to use their geographical and historical knowledge to inform their final regeneration scheme.

5. Moreover, they had pinpointed the organising concepts that they wanted to help develop in the two subjects. For geography, again, this was about a sense of place and a sense of space. The unit of work clearly helped the students understand what this place was like, why this place was like it was, and how and why it had changed. It also helped them understand where and why places are located. For history this piece of work was clearly about change and continuity and causation. By using the maps the pupils saw change happen over time and they pinpointed roughly when the change occurred. They also later on worked out why the area had changed.

6. The teachers had also thought about the processes which they were going to teach this unit of work through. The cross-curricular approach was partly made through enquiry. We will discuss in more detail how enquiry can be used as a tool for cross-curricular learning in Chapter 4. In this example enquiry was clearly used to organise the learning. Historical and geographical enquiry are processes that, in the 2008 National Curriculum, appear to be very similar. In this example the pupils were asking 'geographical questions, thinking critically constructively and creatively'. They also 'analysed and evaluated evidence, presenting findings to draw and justify conclusions'. From a historical viewpoint they were asked to 'identify and investigate, individually and as part of a team, specific historical questions or issues, making and testing hypotheses'. In addition, the work allowed the children to use other subject-specific processes; for history it was the use of historical evidence. They were required to 'identify, select and use a range of historical sources, including textual, visual and oral sources, artefacts and the historic environment'. They also were developing their 'Geogricacy and visual literacy' as they were required to use 'maps at a range of scales [and] photographs'.

7.   The teachers who planned this unit had decided exactly what they wanted the outcomes of the work to be. The end product was a presentation to local dignitaries of how the area could be developed in the future.

8.   They had also prepared the resources well to help the learning develop. The use of photographs, maps and census material was carefully planned and carried out appropriately.

9.   Moreover the activities chosen by the teachers had been thought through and were used to engage the class and develop their understanding. The teacher was therefore also able to develop certain competences which complemented but did not replace the geographical and historical focus.

Two more points have been added to the nine principles above, mentioned by Woodcock (2010), which are well worth considering when planning and teaching a cross-curricular project, namely:

10.   Assessment.

11.   Review.

These 11 points, turned into questions below, can be used when designing cross-curricular humanities work:

1.   How will the cross-curricular links be made? Through content, concepts or both?

2.   How will you ensure that during the project the humanities subjects retain their identity as subjects?

3.   How will you check that you are really allowing subjects that you are not a specialist in to retain their integrity? Will you collaboratively plan the project with an expert from a different subject?

4.   What is it that you actually want to the pupils to achieve?

5.   How will you organise the work? Will you use some of the different organising concepts from the subjects that your project is teaching?

6.   Exactly how will you teach the unit of work? What processes will you use?

7.   What will the outcomes of this unit of work be? How will the pupils show their understanding?

8.   What resources will you use? When and where will you use them in the scheme?

9.   Exactly what teaching activities will you use to develop the pupils' understanding? At what point in the sequence will you deploy them?

10.   How will you assess the work? What exactly is it that you want to assess? Conceptual understanding from individual subjects? Soft skills?

11.   How will review the project? Did the pupils learn what you wanted them to? What would you change in the future?

Reflective task 3.1

Look at the 11 questions/principles above. Some of them can be applied to planning all units of work; some need to be considered when planning cross-curricular work

1. Which of the questions do you think are important to consider when planning any unit of work, either a subject-specific or a cross-curricular project?

2. Which questions do you think are crucial when considering planning a cross-curricular piece of work?

3. Which question do you think might be the most difficult to get right when planning work with another subject in mind?

Clearly these principles can be adhered to when developing and teaching cross-curricular work with two humanities subjects. But this may become more problematic when trying to link more subjects together. How can we ensure that all subjects keep their identity if the content for the humanities work has been chosen arbitrarily by others? All three authors of this book have seen topics such as 'The weather', 'Our island' and 'Slavery' chosen by senior teams and given as the focus of cross-curricular working. But this is where the links can become tenuous and contrived. If a project is going to be meaningful and actually work, it needs the teachers whose subjects are represented to come together at the planning stage to decide on the focus and the approaches used. Inevitably this will take time and thought. The more subjects that come together, the more difficult it will be to get teachers together to talk things through. Moreover, the teachers of each subject need to have a clear understanding of what is in it that is of value to their subject if this work is going to be successful. Wilkinson (2010: 6) suggests that if successful collaboration is going to succeed teachers need to start small:

> The need for 'disciplined curriculum innovation' – in which objectives are clear, and the implementation is both carefully planned and effectively evaluated – almost inevitably means starting small! ... The most effective collaborations are those made between few departments, as and when they are appropriate and genuinely enhance the teaching and learning experience of the students.

It can be argued that when thinking about whether and when to link humanities subjects together or with other subjects across the curriculum, some connect more naturally than others. Often the connection will be made through the chosen content. There are clear connections that can be made between citizenship and other humanities subjects. According to the National Curriculum the study of citizenship should include the 'key features of parliamentary democracy and government in the constituent parts of the UK and at local level, including voting and elections'. This seems to be an ideal starting point for close collaboration with history. After all, the history National Curriculum requires all pupils to be taught 'the development of political power from the Middle Ages to the twentieth century, including changes in the relationship between rulers and ruled over time, the changing relationship between the crown and parliament, and the development of democracy'. It seems sensible, vital even, to teach these topics at a similar point in time, or together, so pupils really can see where democracy has developed from and why we have the system that we now have.

Citizenship also links closely with geography. The study of citizenship should include 'actions that individuals, groups and organisations can take to influence decisions affecting communities and the environment', while the study of geography should include 'interactions between people and their environments, including causes and consequences of these interactions, and how to plan for and manage their future impact'. Links clearly exist between these subjects. But teachers will only see the connections and a coherent approach will only happen if teachers come together and discuss what they are teaching. This takes time and organisation.

Cross-curricular work with other subjects in the curriculum

Many links can be established between the humane subjects and other subjects in the curriculum. Geography for example could link closely with ICT. Geographers need to be able to 'solve problems and make decisions to develop analytical skills and creative thinking about geographical issues'. A requirement for ICT at KS3 is to 'solve problems by developing, exploring and structuring information, and deriving new information for a particular purpose'. The use of ICT databases to help solve geographical problems is an area that many teachers already exploit. Here the ICT and geographical skills are being enhanced. These links are clearly already taking place – but do the teachers involved actually talk to their colleagues who are subject specialists? You may well find by having a discussion with them that you are not teaching how to use the database in the same way or as effectively as your ICT colleagues. The more we can connect to other subjects in our teaching, the more we can help children make links between the subjects – something that pupils are notoriously bad at. Simple phrases like 'Last week in ICT you created your own database to ... search and sort information; well today we are going to use a similar database to search and sort information' can help with this. But without having the conversation with our colleagues we will never know if such links are already there. Nor will we be able to exploit these links and maybe plan some closer cross-curricular work.

History seems to link quite naturally to art and design; for example, paintings make excellent source material. Unlocking their messages can reveal a huge amount about a time period and the artist's viewpoint. This skill is also beneficial to art and design because teachers are required to help their students understand the role of the artist, craftsperson and designer in a range of cultures, times and contexts. Analysing Tudor paintings, Hogarth's prints or Turner's landscapes really helps develop historical and artistic understanding. Are history and art teachers using the same techniques and language in their classrooms? If they are, then this again can help pupils see the connections that exist between subjects. If we are not having such discussions with our colleagues, how will we ever know?

All of the humane subjects are closely linked with English. When analysing texts in RE, history and geography, teachers should help pupils to demonstrate 'a secure understanding of the conventions of written language, including grammar, spelling and punctuation'. Also in RE and history, teachers should be helping their classes explore, 'how ideas, experiences and values are portrayed differently in texts from a range of cultures and traditions'. Indeed this is a rich area for cross-curricular work, particularly between citizenship, RE and science, as pupils can all debate the moral issues scientific developments raise.

Conclusion

For teaching and learning in cross-curricular humanities to be effective, teachers of the humane subjects first have to understand exactly what their own subjects comprise in terms of substantive knowledge and in conceptual understanding. This will allow them to uphold the integrity of their individual subjects in the planning and delivery of cross-curricular work. This is one of the key messages of the book. If teachers are unclear what constitutes their own subjects, then inevitably the losers will be the pupils they teach. One important element in taking a cross-curricular approach is to help develop the citizenship, geography, history and RE 'chips' in children's brains. Teachers also need to be given the time and space to work collaboratively with their colleagues to plan for meaningful and exciting classroom experiences. Teachers need to be clear about the purpose and scope of the work they are planning. Whether projects are enforced from above or germinated from below, teachers need to have ownership of the projects that they develop. If not they might be doomed to failure. However, if teachers talk to their colleagues more about what their subject is and how they are teaching their classes, more and more natural links seem to appear between the subjects. This dialogue can form the starting point of something truly exciting.

Professional standards for QTS

QTS standards: Q10, Q14, Q15, Q22, Q25, Q29, Q32.

Professional standards for teachers

Core standards: C10, C15, C16, C26, C29, C30, C35, C36, C40.

4

Promoting enquiry and independent learning

Key objectives

By the end of this chapter, you will have:

- explored definitions of enquiry and independent learning in the humanities and beyond;
- weighed the desirability or otherwise of using a common definition of enquiry and independent learning to support cross-curricular learning;
- considered how practical examples from case studies show ways that a shared understanding of these definitions can be reached and applied to curriculum planning and a shared language and methodology in classroom practice;
- examined the tensions in using structure to develop independence;
- engaged in a range of reflective and practical tasks which will help you apply key ideas in this chapter to your own teaching practice.

Teachers in most subjects, humane or otherwise, frequently refer to (and often bemoan the lack of) an independent approach to learning amongst pupils. As a process, enquiry and independent learning is perhaps the most obvious starting point for cross-curricular planning, as we all appear to 'do it'. Therefore, a common approach would appear to be sensible and desirable. However, an important first consideration is whether or not we are actually talking about the same thing. In Chapter 2 we broke enquiry down into different areas: asking questions/identifying issues, action planning, seeking and using resources, organising and communicating information, evaluating what has been done and setting targets. For each strand, progression can be seen as growing independence, from teacher direction to pupils being completely autonomous. A more detailed exploration of this is now required to explore the potential of cross-curricular work on enquiry.

Can there be a common approach to enquiry?

There is no widely accepted definition of the process of enquiry or independent learning within the teaching profession. Rather, each subject has created its own definition, and more recently models have emerged based around theories of learning and associated curriculum models. The introduction of the National Curriculum engendered a debate in some subject areas about the core processes of their subjects, yet despite its various revisions it is only in its 2008 version that a common definition has been approached, through the Personal, Learning and Thinking Skills (PLTS) framework. Within this, 'independent enquiry' is identified as an essential skill 'that will enable young people to enter work and adult life as confident and capable individuals' (DCSF/QCA, 2007). It defines this skill as:

Focus:
Young people process and evaluate information in their investigations, planning what to do and how to go about it. They take informed and well-reasoned decisions, recognising that others have different beliefs and attitudes.

Young people:
- identify questions to answer and problems to resolve, plan and carry out research, appreciating the consequences of decisions;
- explore issues, events or problems from different perspectives;
- analyse and evaluate information, judging its relevance and value;
- consider the influence of circumstances, beliefs and feelings on decisions and events;
- support conclusions, using reasoned arguments and evidence.

(DCSF/QCA, 2007)

In isolation, this definition is lacking in several aspects. Fortunately, however, it is not designed to be used in isolation and such important elements as teamwork and cooperative learning are picked up in the other five PLTS.

There is little evidence yet of this becoming a commonly used model, although PLTS is increasingly prevalent in schools so this is liable to change. As the 2008 Ofsted report 'Curriculum innovation in schools' demonstrated, schools have tended to follow different models, with mixed results. This may be because of the non-statutory nature of PLTS within the National Curriculum, and also because most subjects remain preoccupied with their own disciplines rather than looking for a wider definition. Understandably, many school's starting points will also be their own context, which will then define the shape of the curriculum aims, rather than a given framework.

So, whilst it may be tempting to leap at the PLTS definition as a useful basis for a common approach, it is crucial that an understanding of the current definitions in individual subject disciplines is considered alongside this, and furthermore the other definitions currently in play from broader theories of learning and curriculum models. Developing links from existing practice will ensure that current good practice is built upon and that misconceptions and ineffective practice are identified. Indeed, it could be argued that any attempt to create a cross-curricular approach will in itself lead to a less rigorous approach to learning. For example, Erricker (2010) has recently argued that the PLTS approach of cross-curricular skills is fundamentally flawed:

> Of itself, this provides no rigour and does not pay specific attention either to enquiry-based learning or the need to attend to disciplinary requirements of skills progression, specific to subject disciplines, or a conceptual focus or foci on which to base the enquiries.

Instead, he argues for the use of an interdisciplinary approach, distinct from cross-curricular learning in that it:

> demands that the integrity of the discipline is maintained and that skills and conceptual focus are paramount. These are the principles that determine how following more than one discipline in an enquiry can, potentially, be more educationally enriching than learning through separate and discrete disciplines. It follows that interdisciplinary enquiry is only worthwhile if the enquiry itself demands more than one discipline in order to be sufficient and meaningful and relevant for students. Therefore, when conceiving interdisciplinary enquiry it may be that certain obvious areas of the curriculum as it stands obviously lend themselves to it or that new, relevant areas for enquiry suggest themselves.
>
> (Erricker, 2010: 204)

Seeing this as a matter of 'areas' of the curriculum could lead to planning becoming more about content than processes and the skills that serve them, putting the needs of a subject over the needs of a pupil. However, Erricker's contention that this is likely to be more educationally enriching is a powerful one. In either case, understanding how each of the humanities subjects defines the process of enquiry is a crucial step in moving towards a common definition.

As discussed in Chapter 1, there is substantial common ground between citizenship, geography and history. In all three, students are expected to plan enquiries, identify areas of investigation, gather data or information, analyse this critically, and present and justify their findings. It is in the field of study that the differences become more apparent, with history rooted in the past whilst geography and citizenship tend to be based on more contemporary and topical issues.

In history the definition of enquiry has shifted considerably in recent years. In the early versions of the National Curriculum programme of study (DfE, 1995; DfEE/QCA, 1999) enquiry was explicitly linked to the use and evaluation of historical sources, causing it to be seen as about 'using sources' rather than a process in itself. A broader definition was formulated in the late 1990s. Gorman (1998) made the case for a structured approach to enquiry in which careful planning for progression ensured pupils moved to greater independence. He saw the skills of identifying and evaluating sources as part of a broader skill set that included the ability to collect and record information, reach and communicate conclusions, and ask significant questions. Riley (2000) developed this further by laying out clear planning principles for enquiry, centered on the 'carefully crafted enquiry question' (p.8). Riley's ideas have informed thinking on the process of enquiry, including the 2007 National Curriculum programme of study for history (DCSF/QCA, 2007) in which, distinct from a now separately defined process of 'using evidence', it is defined as a process in its own right, in which pupils should be able to 'a) identify and investigate, individually and as part of a team, specific historical questions or issues, making and testing hypotheses; b) reflect critically on historical questions or issues' (p.114). Burnham (2007) has further developed this, seeing pupils developing their own enquiry questions as the most important step towards making enquiry truly independent. Bates, Herrity and McFahn (2009) have developed principles for planning longer enquiries, believing that 'planning longer enquiries provides students with a series of lessons in which they have time to develop these processes more effectively' (p.16). These principles give an articulation of the whole enquiry process, the clearest definition yet.

The advantages of the 'enquiry sequence' have been increasingly recognised in geography teaching since Roberts (2003) identified four essential aspects of enquiry work in geography (creating a need to know, using data, making sense, reflecting). Taylor (2008) further developed this in the light of concepts being explicitly included in the geography National Curriculum programme of study (DCSF/QCA, 2007) alongside the key process of 'geographical enquiry'. This states that:

Pupils should be able to:
1. ask geographical questions, thinking critically, constructively and creatively
2. collect, record and display information
3. identify bias, opinion and abuse of evidence in sources when investigating issues
4. analyse and evaluate evidence, presenting findings to draw and justify conclusions
5. find creative ways of using and applying geographical skills and understanding to create new interpretations of place and space
6. plan geographical enquiries, suggesting appropriate sequences of investigation
7. solve problems and make decisions to develop analytical skills and creative thinking about geographical issues.

(DCSF/QCA, 2007: 104)

Although there are clear parallels with the history equivalent, the separation of the use of evidence has not taken place in the same way. This leaves a less precise definition – Taylor builds on Riley (2000) in her work to emphasise the centrality of the good enquiry question and the 'enquiry sequence' that serves this, but in conclusion admits that she is contributing to a 'lively debate about enquiry, big concepts, key concepts, and maybe even organising concepts in geography' (Taylor, 2008: 53). A fair inference might be that the debate is less developed amongst geography teachers than in history, albeit proceeding upon similar lines. However there does seem to be much agreement in the literature that an enquiry should be seen as a whole approach to teaching and learning, in contrast to the view in history that it is one of several equally useful approaches.

The view in RE is far less clear, a symptom largely of the fact that it has not generally been viewed as a subject discipline by its teachers, and therefore requires greater

61

exploration. History teachers often refer in their lessons to developing the skills of a historian. The tendency in RE has been quite different and often diverse, avoiding higher levels skills such as evaluation (Erricker, 2010). Given that a common view of the subject has not been developed through the National Curriculum, the imperative to shape a common view has not existed in the same way as for many other subjects. Erricker sees conceptual enquiry as 'the basis for the construction of learning and teaching'. However, Erricker makes it clear that his views are intended as a radical revision of current orthodoxy in RE teaching nationally rather than building on a widely held view, commenting that: 'we need to go back to educational principles that can justify the subject's curriculum time.' Certainly there are many RE teachers who would take a less radical view.

Reflective task 4.1

It is clear that common ground exists between the humanities subjects. Indeed, the debates have cross-fertilised each other over the years. To what extent could the humanities subjects in your school approach enquiry in different ways? Talking to colleagues in other subject areas could reveal commonalities you were not aware of and also important differences.

A useful activity is to choose a common topic, such as the Holocaust, climate change or population growth, and ask what key enquiry question each subject would use. Test these against the following criteria (from Riley, 2000):

Does each of your enquiry questions:
- Capture the interest and imagination of your pupils?
- Place an aspect of thinking, concept or process at the forefront of the pupils' minds?
- Result in a tangible, lively, substantial, enjoyable 'outcome activity' (i.e. at the end of the lesson sequence) through which pupils can genuinely answer the enquiry question?

An examination of a case study that has proved successful in developing enquiry will help us to explore the challenge of taking a cross-curricular approach.

Case study 4.1: *Battalion 101: Why did they shoot?*

In this case study, a history teacher describes his approach to the planning and delivery of a lesson that was taught by a range of teachers on a cross-curricular citizenship day, exploring difference and diversity through the Holocaust.

Quite rightly, the focus for most Holocaust teaching is on the victims. However, when teaching this difficult area I have always felt that a closer look at the perpetrators is important. After all, if one of our aims in Holocaust education is to ensure it never happens again, we need to understand something of the killers' motivation in carrying out such terrible acts. My approach to this has been to look in depth at just one small group. In this way, I hope to avoid sweeping statements that can so often lead to ill-informed generalisations – 'They were all brainwashed', 'They were just following orders.' It is unfair to expect 14-year-olds to gain a full understanding of the complexities of such an issue, but that does not mean they cannot engage with the issue on a smaller scale. In order to achieve this I chose to focus on the activities of Reserve Police Battalion 101 in Poland during 1942/3. We know much about this group due to the research of Christopher Browning in his 1992 book *Ordinary Men* and the academic debate that followed its publication.

The lesson began with pupils being read a description of a mass execution by an *Einsatzgruppe*. Their attention was drawn to the attitude of the executioners, one of whom, amidst the bodies, 'sat, legs swinging, on the edge of the ditch. He had an automatic rifle. He was smoking a cigarette.' This immediately led us into the objectives of the session, to explore why people would behave in this way, and how we should respond to this. After providing some brief historical context of the Nazi period, the path to the Holocaust and the role of the SS, we focused on the use of reserve police battalions as the killings became too widespread for the SS alone. Having introduced Battalion 101 as 'ordinary' Hamburg men, average age 39, of mixed backgrounds, only 25 per cent Nazi party members, I revealed to the pupils their crimes – 38,000 Jews murdered in a 16-month period, a further 48,000 sent to death camps. We then looked at a detailed description of their first 'special action' in the Polish village of Jozefow, accompanied by images of their actions on this day. How could apparently 'ordinary men' behave in such a way?

I then introduced to the pupils 16 cards that contained possible reasons for their actions. These ranged from simplistic explanations such as 'They were mad' to more complex ideas such as 'They believed that they had no choice. If they refused to do it, they might be shot.' Pupils organised these cards onto a line of significance to show the extent to which they thought these reasons influenced their actions. Most pupils laid heavy emphasis on the idea of compulsion and fear. I then began to drip-feed in pieces of evidence from Browning's research to eventually show that they were given the option by their commander not to participate in the killings, but still the majority chose to continue. As this evidence emerged, pupils were constantly revising their thinking through moving the cards. It became clear that the reservists' motivation was complex and difficult to understand from a modern day perspective. The reasons for the actions of Battalion 101 could not easily be explained. This led to the wider point that only through rigorous study of the Holocaust can we possibly achieve the mission of ensuring it never happens again. Lazy stereotypes are not good enough.

Finally we examined the fate of the members of Battalion 101. The pupils were shocked to discover that very few were punished, even when their crimes were fully investigated at a trial in Hamburg in 1967. To finish we looked at the true story of 'Simon and the SS guard'. This tells the story of a Holocaust survivor who is confronted by the confession of a dying SS guard. The guard asks for forgiveness. The pupils were asked to reflect silently on whether they thought Simon would forgive him and then share their response – before revealing that in reality he refused.

Reflective task 4.2

What aspects of enquiry does this promote? This case study, although delivered by subject specialists from across the humanities, is predominantly history based. How might RE and citizenship approach the same material?

A common approach to enquiry?

We could infer from the above overview that the basis for a common approach exists. The centrality of the enquiry question, the importance of evaluating evidence, and the need to have a clear outcome linked to the question are all identified as features of good enquiry work across the subjects. There are definite benefits to adopting a common approach across subjects, not least for the beleaguered pupil experiencing five or six different subjects a day, many of which may well be asking for engagement in the process of enquiry but in different ways, through different stages and with different language. However, as discussed in Chapter 1, when looking at competency-based curricula such as the RSA's 'Opening Minds' a focus on enquiry purely as a process will have even less meaning for a pupil unless specific contexts exist. The trick therefore is to find a happy medium between the two that will have relevance and meaning for the pupil, but also provide rigour and lead to progress in the subjects involved. Choosing the right area of study therefore becomes far more important than a model process. Hence, whilst we certainly *could* take a common approach to enquiry, it is far more important to consider whether we *should*, and if so when and how.

A common approach to enquiry is clearly possible. The subjects have enough common ground to explore this fruitfully, and these case studies show that collaboration can have a positive impact on learning above that which might be possible through subjects working in isolation. To explore the practicalities of such an approach, the following case study explores how three departments within a humanities faculty addressed the possibility of using a common approach to enquiry.

Case study 4.2: *Should a common approach be adopted?*

In this school the subjects are taught separately at KS3 and at KS4, with approximately 60 per cent of pupils each year studying one or more. However, most of the staff teach more than one subject and all teach citizenship. There cross-curricular working was already an established practice. The Head of His has read the work of Bates, Herrity and McFahn (2009) referred to above and ιeιt their principles for planning longer enquiries might form the basis of a common approach across the humanities subjects. To test this assumption, he interviewed both the geography and RE subject leaders, having already given them copies of these principles as a stimulus for further debate:

1. Students genuinely investigate for themselves.
2. There will be some elements of students raising their own questions/ hypotheses.
3. They use authentic sources – even if in modified form.
4. There is an element of the enquiry being contentious.
5. There is a coherence to the way the enquiry progresses.
6. Understanding key concepts (and the later consolidation of this) must be an integral part of the planning.
7. The guiding problematic enquiry question is referred to frequently in each lesson. Questioning needs to be carefully planned to allow access to higher-level reasoning.
8. There is a balance between structured support and open-ended research. There must always be an element of students working on their own ideas.
9. There should be some new injection of evidence, possibly contradictory to their earlier sources, to simulate the reality of historical research and to encourage students to react to it. How does it fit with their emerging view? How should they respond?
10. There must be an element of students evaluating other accounts, either from other students or historical interpretations: visual, audio and text media.
11. Students arrive at an independent conclusion, forming their own judgement. This should be a product which commits students to creating an answer, i.e. making history.

(From Bates, Herrity and McFahn, 2009)

When asked to explain what he felt was meant by enquiry, the geography subject leader replied that there were conflicting views of enquiry amongst geography teachers in that, whilst a 'whole approach' might be seen as desirable, in reality there is a mixture of this and the use of it as one of a number of processes. The emphasis on the centrality of key questions directly mirrors the literature (Riley, 2000; Taylor, 2008). The interviewee also reflected on the fact that this inconsistency exists both in his own department and also more widely in the geography teaching community, stating:

> I think it is going to vary between viewpoints and different understandings of it. I think the basics of looking at places and processes and interaction are going to be there.

Although recognising that he was not in a position to comment authoritatively on the wider picture in the county or nationally, he did conclude that these differences may not be so much a philosophical divide as one born from different eras of teacher training and experience. A more 'traditional' approach was characterised as: 'This is what you have to find out and this is where you can find it – off you go,' whereas a more modern approach might be a 'personal approach, what they understand about that place and where they want to take it'. This reflects the approach outlined in the PLTS framework with its emphasis on 'pupils planning what to do and how to go about it' (QCA, 2007). Given these quite different approaches any plans for a common approach would clearly need to invest significantly and at an early stage in professional development that enables a shared understanding. A 'received' version of enquiry, no matter how well reasoned, researched and tied into current statutory frameworks, will clearly not be sufficient to ensure a consistent approach in the classroom when it is being delivered by staff with these divergent approaches.

A further reflection on these differing attitudes was linked to resources. A barrier to moving to a whole approach was related to resources in that:

> 'in an ideal world if you had infinite resources with laptops and all the different things you could do, then it makes it a lot easier to have a geographical enquiry in every lesson.'
> 'So resources might be a barrier to achieving this?'
> 'Yes – I think it certainly would be easier today if we had in every geography class a computer for each pupil; then they can go away, they can do their research, research GIS and all these things which formulate a key part of it.'

This takes us back to the question of 'could we' use a common approach, but not from the point of view of differing views about pedagogy. Rather it is seen as an issue of having the right resources. This could be seen as an ambitious subject leader taking advantage of the fact that he has a chance to make a case for more departmental resources – certainly an approach used by many subject leaders when in the same position! However it does demonstrate another aspect of any future plans, in that moving to such an approach will have a resource implication that may necessarily limit the scope of changes.

The RE subject leader's answers similarly backed the conclusion drawn earlier in this chapter, in that far less consensus exists on what is meant by enquiry. Clearly influenced by the work of Clive Erricker, he was able to explain the process of conceptual enquiry and how this was applied to the current RE syllabus in his department. Growing independence is again seen as a key characteristic of progression, in that pupils are developing their own views and evaluating those of others.

Again concerns about an inconsistent approach surface here. Whilst schemes of work may show this model of enquiry is well understood and planned by the subject leader, a shared understanding across the team of teachers is a challenge:

> I think that it is being slowly embedded at the moment. So – the schemes of work – we are rewriting them now so this year we have worked specifically and had in bold at the top 'Apply or Communicate' – so they know which stage they are on. I would probably suggest that if you asked any of the team 'Do you really understand this in as much detail as we would hope?' – we are not at that stage yet but that is something we are working on.

This answer demonstrates the specific challenges faced by RE leaders. In common with most RE departments, the team is made up of only two specialist teachers, with the remainder being non-specialists, albeit mostly from within the humanities team. This is compounded by the fact that nationally no consensus exists, nor is there a requirement for this through a national curriculum. However this comment does also demonstrate a commitment to work with these teachers and provide the necessary support. Therefore it could be assumed that in any attempt to introduce a common approach, there is already a commitment to develop staff, albeit in a top-down way.

When analysing the common approach, which was given to both interviewees one week in advance of the interviews, both reacted in a generally positive way. Both saw clear benefits for pupils in such an approach and identified in particular that for pupils it would allow them to transfer learning much more effectively from one subject to another. In particular the need for greater learner independence was seen as a key benefit, with the RE subject leader commenting that such an approach would lead to pupils being able to:

> transfer those across to other subjects and other areas of their lives as well rather than that idea of them being spoon fed – or them always looking to a teacher or an adult for an answer rather than wanting to find out for themselves.

Interestingly neither saw this approach as a threat to their subject area. Indeed the geography subject leader saw this as a means by which it might be strengthened:

> I think it also gives them a better understanding of what geography is, because if they have adopted an approach, as we were talking about, looking at sources and the evaluation of those sources, well is that as relevant in geography as it is in history?

By highlighting the similarities between approaches it also enables pupils to draw out where the differences exist and to help them understand 'what geography is about'.

In both cases no major threats were perceived. The expectation was that flexibility would be given and therefore a department could still decide where the best place would be to apply such an approach.

Both interviewees saw specific parts of the suggested common approach that might need adjustment in order to take this from a history-specific approach to one that could be effectively applied across all three subjects. In some cases this focused on terminology rather than pedagogy. For example, when looking at 'authentic sources' these might be quite different in nature but the principle of using engaging material, which could also be seen as 'contentious' and thus tie in with point 4 of the common approach, was seen as important once the discussion had clarified this.

Another specific part of the common approach that was seen as potentially problematic was point 11: forming an independent conclusion. This may have been simply because of the use of the phrase 'making history'. Once the discussion developed beyond this it became clear that for both interviewees it came down to pupils forming their own views and then being able to back these up, and at higher levels apply them to different contexts. Interestingly the geography subject leader also drew a parallel with scientific methodology, especially in the use of data, as an example of where the links may not always most obviously sit within the humanities subjects.

Finally point 9 was highlighted as an area in need of some development. Again this may simply be that the use of a specific phrase, in this case 'the reality of historical research', caused some concern. However when it became clear through discussion that what was really intended was to focus on a rigorous thought process, this was felt to be less of an issue, although in both interviews this was left as inconclusive and would need further development.

These interviews highlighted the challenges of working with a diverse team and the need for a consensus to be built on a common approach, which would be an essential first step in this process. This would not be primarily about 'getting the wording right'. This in itself could be quite easily agreed between subject leaders. However, without the ownership of this approach by the broader team, it would take the form of an imposed structure being introduced into a broader team that did not have a shared view. Hence the chances of this having a positive impact on pupils would be low.

The history subject leader felt these interviews established that a common approach to enquiry could be established. No fundamental barriers to this in terms of either subject pedagogy or staff attitudes existed, although there were significant implications for staff training. This was not felt to indicate that a common approach could not be introduced, simply that it would take longer and need a greater investment of resources. Therefore, to develop this further, it was necessary to begin with a broad training programme for all humanities staff that would engage them with a common approach to enquiry as it stands and enable them to play a full part in its revision. Once agreement was reached on this and future resourcing could be secured, it was then believed to be possible to agree a curriculum structure through which this could be implemented, leading to a longitudinal study of its impact upon pupil attitudes and progress. Despite the challenges identified, this faculty felt they could and would use a common approach to the process of enquiry in the humanities.

Reflective task 4.3

How would your humanities colleagues react to a common approach to enquiry? In this case study a researched model was presented as a starting point. Would you use this approach to start a debate, or is it better to collectively agree a model from scratch?

What would subsequent staff development need to look like to achieve the 'buy in' discussed in Chapter 2?

How detailed should the planning for a common approach be? There is an important balance to be struck between, on the one hand, being over prescriptive and alienating colleagues and, on the other hand, being so loose that any sense of rigorous interdisciplinary working is lost.

This case study uses a common approach that arises from the history teaching subject community. Of course models have arisen from the other humanities subjects. The two examples in Table 4.1 and Figure 4.1 below could equally be used as a starting point for a common approach to enquiry.

Table 4.1 'Geographical Enquiry and Progression in Teaching Styles' (Telfer, 2000 adapted from Roberts 1996), by kind permission of Steve Telfer

Stage of teaching and learning	Closed	Framed	Negotiated
Questions	Questions not explicit or questions remain the teacher's questions.	Questions explicit, activities planned to make children ask questions.	Children decide what they want to investigate under guidance from teacher.
Data	Data selected by teacher, presented as authoritative, not to be challenged.	Variety of data selected by teacher, presented as evidence to be interpreted.	Children are helped to find their own data from sources in and out of school.
Interpretation	Teacher decides what is to be done with data, children follow instructions.	Methods of interpretation are open to discussion and choice.	Children chose methods of analysis and interpretation in consultation with teacher.
Conclusion	Key ideas presented, generalisations are predicted, not open to debate.	Children reach conclusions from data, different interpretations are expected.	Children reach their own conclusions and evaluate them.
Summary	Teacher controls the knowledge by making all decisions about data, activities, conclusions. Children are not expected to challenge what is presented.	The teacher inducts children into ways in which geographical knowledge is constructed, so that they are able to use these ways to construct knowledge themselves. Children are made aware of choices and are encouraged to become critical.	Children are enabled by the teacher to investigate questions of concern and interest to themselves.

Source: Telfer, 2004, adapted from Roberts (2003).

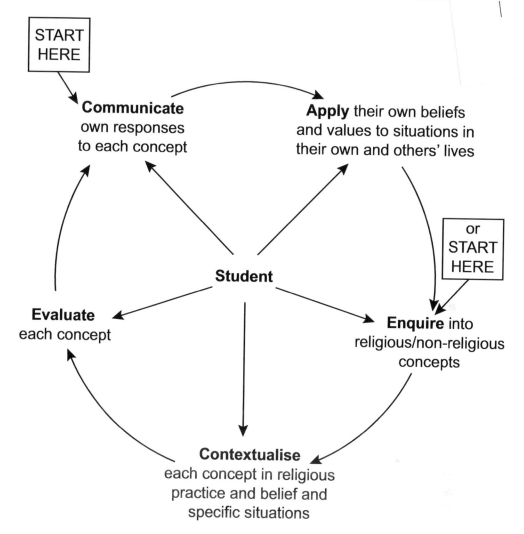

Figure 4.1 'Enquiry and Skills – a methodology for teaching and learning in RE' (Erricker 2010), copyright Hampshire County Council, permission given by Clive Erricker on the basis of licensed agreement with Hampshire County Council

---

Reflective task 4.4

How would the response to the previous reflective task differ if your colleagues were presented with the models shown in Table 4.1 and Figure 4.1?

What are the common elements across all three models? Does this provide a basis for a common approach to enquiry in the humanities in itself? What might be the opportunities presented by such an approach? What might be the threats?

Using rigorous enquiry questions to lead learning: less detail, more meaning?

Whatever your response to the above reflective tasks, it will be clear that such a common approach runs the risk of leading teachers too far away from their subject disciplines. The dangers of this have already been outlined in the opening two chapters of this book and will be returned to in the concluding one. An approach that leaves different subjects, humanities or otherwise, more open to making meaningful links from their own subject discipline is through the use of rigorous enquiry questions.

Andrew Wrenn (2010) has provided some good examples of this approach. Starting with an example of an imposed theme to which all subjects might be expected to contribute in a school, he shows subjects might at least make the best of this through the use of stepped enquiry questions. For example, taking the topic 'Volcanoes' he offers the suggestions shown in Figure 4.2 (garnered from subject advisers).

Of course, Wrenn accepts this is very much a case of making the best of a poor model. Yet the conclusions he draws demonstrate that there is value in this approach. Firstly he notes that simply by going through this process, no matter how ill conceived in the first place, unexpected overlaps and links between subjects emerged. Simply having the conversation enabled the development of useful cross-curricular thinking. Of course not all are useful. The PE and MFL examples are clearly spurious. Secondly he notes that even where the theme appears superficial the medium to short-term planning that accompanies it can still result in something rigorous and engaging. The theme is not a barrier to this, especially in subjects such as music and English where there is little in the way of prescribed content or substantive knowledge.

However the choice of a potentially sensitive theme, the Holocaust, raises further and more serious questions (see Figure 4.3).

The barriers to teaching sensitive and controversial topics and practical ways in which these can be overcome are explored in depth in Chapter 6. What is clear from looking at these questions is that, whilst they might be perfectly valid enquiry questions, teacher and pupil would need to understand the historical context to be able to engage effectively and appropriately with them. This is where genuinely interdisciplinary work is essential in order to, as Wrenn states, 'bring out the coherence and problematic areas of the thinking process which is the characteristic of each discipline'.

PE
- What effect would a volcanic eruption have on community sport?
- What kind of sport would be possible in a refugee camp?
- Can we create a set of rules for a new ball game in a refugee camp?

MATHEMATICS
- How can we present the effects of a volcanic eruption through graphs?
- What can graphs tell us about the volcanic eruption in X?
- How do the graphs from eruption X and eruption Y differ?

GEOGRAPHY
- What can Pliny's letter tell us about volcanic eruptions?
- How much did the 1883 Krakatoa eruption change the island?
- How much have volcanoes changed the landscape around the world?

SCIENCE
- How did Mount St Helens change our knowledge about volcanoes?
- Can we use science to stop people dying in eruptions?
- How do we know how volcanoes behave on other planets?

CITIZENSHIP
- Why do some people live while others die in volcanic eruptions?
- What rights should people living near a volcano expect?
- Should foreign people help when an eruption happens somewhere else? If so, why and who should pay?

VOLCANOES

RE
- How did ordinary Romans react to dying in Pliny's letter?
- How have religions explained volcanoes and the deaths they cause?
- Is it fair to blame these deaths on God?

DESIGN AND TECHNOLOGY
- How do websites use software to animate volcanic eruptions?
- Which are the most effective examples of animated eruptions?
- Why are they better than others?
- How can we use software to create an animation of an eruption?

ART AND DESIGN
- How have artists drawn and painted volcanoes?
- Why do artists draw and paint volcanoes differently?
- How will I choose to paint or draw an eruption?

HISTORY
- What can archaeology tell us about Pompeii?
- What can Pliny's letter tell us about Pompeii?
- What can Pompeii tell us about the Romans?

ENGLISH
- What can Pliny's letter tell us about him and the Romans?
- What can a website on volcanoes tell us about the people who wrote it?
- What can *Dante's Peak* tell us about its filmmaker?
- How should I present my newspaper story about a volcanic eruption?

MUSIC
- How do film scores describe natural disasters?
- How does *Dante's Peak*'s score describe a volcanic eruption?
- What features of a volcanic eruption should we include in our composition?
- Which musical elements best describe these features?

ICT
- What can websites tell us about the effects of a volcanic eruption?
- How can we present the effects of a volcanic eruption through software?

MFL
- How does a German website describe volcanoes?
- What German words do I need to label a volcano?
- Can I use these words to describe a volcanic eruption?

Source: Wrenn, 2010: 34.

Figure 4.2 'An example of how different subjects might contribute to a cross-curricular focus on volcanoes' (Andrew Wrenn), by kind permission of The Historical Association

DESIGN AND TECHNOLOGY
- What different kinds of memorials to the Holocaust are there?
- Are these memorials likely to make people think or feel differently about the same events?
- If so, how does the design and use of materials do this?
- What should I put in my memorial design for our school?

RE
- Where does anti-Semitism come from?
- How did people keep a religious faith during the Holocaust?
- How could God have allowed it to happen?

MFL
- What can we tell about Anne Frank from extracts from her diary?
- What vocabulary will we need to create a storyboard of her life?

MATHEMATICS
- How can we depict the distances travelled by Holocaust victims in 1939?
- How did these distances change between 1941 and 1942?
- How did these distances change between 1943 and 1945?

HOLOCAUST

PE
- How did Jesse Owens disprove Nazi racism?
- How can we fight racism in sport today?

MUSIC
- How was music used by the Nazis during the Holocaust?
- What different music has been inspired by the Holocaust?
- What music can we create in memory of the Holocaust?

HISTORY
- Why did the Nazis persecute Jews?
- Who were responsible for the Final Solution?
- Why did the Allies not bomb Auschwitz?
- How should the Holocaust be remembered?

ART AND DESIGN
- What kind of art did Samuel Bak create during the Holocaust?
- What can we tell from the art of Samuel Bak created after the Holocaust?
- What can I put in my picture about the Holocaust in the style of Samuel Bak?

CITIZENSHIP
- What is genocide?
- Is genocide happening in Darfur today?
- What is being done about Darfur?
- Can genocide be stopped?

GEOGRAPHY
- What were the sites of Auschwitz, Dachau and Bergen-Belsen like before 1933?
- How and why did the Holocaust change these sites?
- How do local people relate to Auschwitz, Dachau and Bergen-Belsen today?
- Can we predict what might happen to these sites in the future?

SCIENCE
- What scientific claims did the Nazis make about their ideas?
- How scientific were Nazi claims about race?
- What does modern science tell us about differences between people?

ICT
- Where can I find information about the Holocaust?
- How do I know I can trust what websites say about the Holocaust?
- What information should go into a Wikipedia entry on the Holocaust?

ENGLISH
- What kind of poetry was written during the Holocaust?
- How was the poetry written about the Holocaust after 1945 different?
- What kind of poems can I write about the Holocaust?

Source: Wrenn, 2010: 35.

Figure 4.3 'An example of how different subjects might contribute to a cross-curricular focus on the Holocaust' (Andrew Wrenn), by kind permission of The Historical Association

A common way ahead?

In this chapter we have explored the context for teachers' understanding of enquiry and independent learning, and used several case studies to examine the challenges and opportunities provided by attempting a cross-curricular approach to this. As has been the case in the previous three chapters, what emerges is the importance of building such

Practical task 4.1

1. Wrenn's work arose initially from supporting colleagues who found themselves presented with arbitrarily chosen topics that subjects had to fit into. The authors of this book have encountered several such topics in their work with different schools. Favourites include 'Kenya', 'Water', 'Forests' and 'In the land of the red squirrel'. Choose one of these, or one of your own, and approach colleagues in other subjects to come up with enquiry questions for this from their own subject disciplines.

   To what extent does this generate the valuable discourse Wrenn suggests is possible from even the most absurd topic? Do ideas about the medium to short-term planning that might arise from this suggest genuinely meaningful learning experiences can arise?

2. Given the choice, what might be a genuinely useful topic of study around which the humanities subjects might structure a series of enquiry questions? One example might be the Amazonian rainforest. Another might be the idea of Atonement. Are there others that could be generated from a discussion with humanities colleagues?

approaches from a well-founded understanding of one's own subject discipline. An effective common approach as such does not exist, and perhaps it should not. By definition, such an approach moves us away from the principles outlined in the opening two chapters of this book, that any such approach requires a level of 'buy in' that has eluded virtually all of those colleagues who have attempted it – the Apple School case study explored in Chapter 2 shows this very clearly. This is not to say that common ground does not exist, and clearly it can be built upon with some potential for success, as the views of subject leaders analysed above show. Taking an aspect such as key enquiry questions and building upon this has the clear potential to develop such thinking. Whether or not it is wise to pursue such approaches will be explored further in the concluding chapter of this book.

Professional standards for QTS

This chapter will help you meet the following Q standards: Q6, Q7a, Q8, Q10, Q14, Q15, Q22, Q32.

Professional standards for teachers

This chapter will help you meet the following core standards: C6, C7, C8, C10, C15, C16, C26, C40.

5

Using talk to support thinking in the humanities

Key objectives

By the end of this chapter, you will have:

- focused on developing the pupils' ability to discuss through exploratory talk and approaches to group work;
- explored the benefits of talk to pupils' learning;
- identified the characteristics of effective talk and practical ways to promote this within the classroom;
- examined the role of teacher talk in motivating pupils and providing challenge and higher-level thinking amongst pupils.

Talk is one of those areas which can easily be neglected yet it provides one of the most powerful ways to support young people's intellectual development and understanding of the world in which they live. Vygotsky saw a direct link between the development of language and thinking, as Wood (1988: 31) explains:

> speech comes to form what Vygotsky referred to as the higher mental processes. These include the ability to plan, evaluate, memorize and reason. ... Looked at in this way, language does not simply *reflect* or represent concepts already formed on a non-verbal level. Rather, it structures and directs the processes of thinking and concept formation themselves.

Consequently a focus on talk and supporting students' ability to talk should see an improvement in their cognitive abilities; language helps students articulate their ideas but also helps to develop those ideas.

Additionally the humanities subjects are particularly suited to a discussion-based teaching approach. This is due to the subject nature – the humanities subjects are not just 'stuff' that has to be learnt; rather the subjects address issues about people, their actions, and their impact on others and the world in which we live. In short there is much to debate; the subjects are not bodies of received knowledge, instead they give rise to questions about *how* we know, *what* we should know, *why* things are the way they are, and what can be done. The subjects provide a rich vein of material that needs mulling over, with contrasting views presented and evaluated along with the difficult issues that need confronting rather than avoiding.

In many ways it is easy to see why talk is often neglected – the overwhelming majority of people can talk, it is something that comes naturally and in some cases teachers often wish certain pupils talked less! However, as with most things, if we want pupils to do something well they need to be taught how to do it, and this applies to talk just as much as to other areas of our teaching.

We do though need to be clear about the different types of talk that occur within a classroom – teacher talk, teacher–pupil talk and pupil–pupil talk – and how each may be developed productively to support learning in the humanities classroom.

In many ways, what follows in this chapter could be applied to any subject as the points can be construed as simply good teaching ideas. This is true, but at the same time they are still valuable, and there are concerns that talk is an underdeveloped aspect of classroom practice. This is a shame, especially in the humanities subjects as they offer a wealth of opportunities for pupils to engage in meaningful debates about the world in which they live and the issues that people have faced and continue to face in society. Geography clearly deals with many pressing issues such as climate change and sustainable development. RE deals with issues of faith but also can draw on philosophical teachings to discuss questions such as poverty. Citizenship is obviously embedded in the current needs and debates in society. Even history, although rooted in the past, raises an insight into many of the issues that have faced people and which still matter today; even silly and seemingly innocuous tales about Roman toilet habits raise serious questions about public health facilities – what should be provided and who should be responsible. We would therefore argue that high-quality classroom talk is central to high-quality learning in the humanities.

Teacher talk (and teacher thinking!)

As Wood (1988: 179) states, 'children need specific kinds of communicative experiences and some external support in order to develop uses of language beyond those demanded by everyday conversation.' In other words, we, as teachers, need to be aware of the specific intellectual demands of the humanities subjects and examine ways to ensure that the talk that is employed supports the development of this thinking. Perhaps 'talk' is not the right word, as we are really focusing on 'thinking' and the ways in which we want young people to think about the subjects – once we are clear about this then we can look at ways to use talk productively.

Although it may sound obvious, teachers need to be clear about what they want to teach, which in recent years has led to an enormous focus on lesson objectives. We are not necessarily fans of lesson objectives being written up on the board at the start of a lesson (sometimes we may want to surprise pupils) nor do we believe that pupils need to write them down at the start of each lesson. However we do believe strongly that as teachers we need to be very clear about what we want pupils to learn and what we want them to think about; in this respect lesson objectives are very important and need to be as precise as possible.

To give an example, let us look at a lesson on flooding, taking a case study of the serious flooding that occurred in Boscastle in 2004. A teacher may reasonably say to the pupils that they will understand why the flooding occurred. Yet this does not get very deeply into the type of thinking the pupils actually need to engage with. Firstly the term 'understand' is very difficult to define – what precisely will the pupils understand? What does understanding look like and how will the teacher check this understanding? 'Understanding' as an objective is not very helpful. Secondly the focus on why something happened, in this case flooding, is yet again not very precise. Pupils may come up with a whole range of answers in response to 'why' – these may be very simple mono-causal answers, or they may be multi-causal, the answer may show how various factors are linked, pupils may categorise the different factors that they identify (these categories may be pupil or teacher determined, and may employ specialist or everyday language), pupils may be required to prioritise the factors and so forth. In other words, as teachers we may want pupils to think in many different ways about why this flooding occurred. Identifying the very precise way in which we want pupils to think is extremely valuable; it allows us, as teachers to be very clear about the learning that will take place, and allows pupils a better chance of properly understanding what they need to learn and of developing a stronger sense of how the subjects operate.

Similarly, in citizenship it may be possible for a teacher to set a lesson objective that pupils will appreciate the complexity of identity. Again there is a problem with the lack of precision of the word 'appreciate'. There is also a need to unpack the idea of complexity and identity further. Pupils may be asked to identify the different identities that they hold, what factors inform a sense of identity, how a sense of identity might change and what circumstances might lead to such a change.

Practical task 5.1

Tables 5.1 and 5.2 provide different ways of approaching the question about the type of thinking teachers may ask students to engage with. Table 5.1, although not exhaustive, identifies different types of thinking.

Think of a lesson you are going to teach in the near future. Examine these descriptions closely in order to:

*   identify those types of thinking that would be most strongly associated with the humanities subjects for this lesson, and whether some are more specific to citizenship, geography, history and RE;

*   identify any types of thinking in this lesson that appear to be missing.

Table 5.1 'Descriptions of thinking', from Saxton and Morgan, *What is History Teaching?* (1994), cited in Husbands (1996), reproduced with the kind permission of Open University Press. All rights reserved

Connecting	Contrasting	Rehearsing	Inducing
Arguing	Projecting	Testing	Approximating
Convincing	Questioning	Clarifying	Selecting
Generating	Reconciling	Reflecting	Deducing
Analysing	Suspending	Judging	Generalising
Capitulating	Wondering	Disrupting	Alluding
Relating	Rejecting	Cooperating	Solving
Composing	Hazarding	Synchronising	Matching
Retracting	Modifying	Harmonising	Probing
Associating	Including	Speculating	Eliciting
Sequencing	Inventing	Contradicting	Soliciting
Suggesting	Extending	Assimilating	Recalling
Sorting	Accommodating	Empathising	Calculating
Imagining	Proving	Compromising	Formulating
Comparing	Hypothesising	Refuting	Valuing
Intuiting	Refining	Internalising	Abstracting
	Predicting	Improving	

Source: from Saxton and Morgan (1994), cited in Husbands (1996).

Practical task 5.2

Table 5.2 lists a range of starter words and phrases for framing lesson objectives.

Considering the same lesson as used for Practical task 5.1, consider how you could:

* apply these to your teaching in to this lesson;

* identify other words and phrases that you could usefully use.

Table 5.2 'Framing history lesson objectives', by kind permission of Christine Counsell

- Does the objective define a learning outcome?
- Will it help you to decide whether the pupils have learned anything at the end of the lesson?
- Is it something that you will be able to see, hear or read? (i.e. you must have a way of checking that you have MET your objectives).

Some useful words and phrases that will give you the precision that you need in a learning objective:

By the end of the lesson pupils will be able to...

select...	classify...
extract...	sort...
give examples of...	arrange...
relate...	justify...
identify...	justify their thinking concerning ...
choose...	explain their thinking concerning...
connect...	compare...
link...	contrast...
make a link between...	define...
explain...	analyse...
illustrate...	join up....
show the relationship between...	shape...
explain the relationship between...	organise...
comment upon...	reconsider...
remember...	support...
recall...	support a view that...
ask questions about...	evaluate...
choose questions that...	weigh...
find...	weigh up...
design...	create...
prioritise...	construct...
create headings...	draw out...

refine headings...	challenge...
challenge headings...	mount a challenge concerning...
limit...	build...
extend...	structure...
amplify...	represent...
judge...	reorganise...
substantiate...	tease out...

Source: University of Cambridge Faculty of Education History PGCE Handbook for Trainees and Mentors 2010–11

Avoid words such as *discuss, complete, fill in, annotate, listen, finish* or *gather.* These are descriptions of procedures, tasks or activities. They are not learning objectives. They are fine for your activities in your lesson plan – but not for your *objectives.* You might legitimately want pupils to 'do the exercise' or 'fill in the chart' or 'complete the exercise' or 'write an essay' or 'listen to the story' or 'do a role-play', but these cannot be described as learning objectives.

Avoid words such as *become aware of, experience, learn about, empathise with* or *understand.* These are too vague for you to assess whether or not learning has taken place. Also, they don't help you with defining what pupils are learning. They are perfectly valid aims and experiences, but your job is to specify the learning outcomes that will demonstrate some headway towards such aims and experiences.

Once the precise nature of the thinking that is being expected has been clearly identified, teachers are in a position to help pupils develop a better understanding of the humanities subjects, as teachers are better able to identify the precise questions that need to be asked to help pupils develop their understanding of the humanities subjects. In this respect questioning becomes vitally important. Many issues related to questioning are generic, regardless of a teacher's subject specialism, but hopefully the following section will allow you to reflect more carefully on how you question pupils.

Problems with questioning

Teachers ask questions for many reasons: to test knowledge, to elicit pupils' 'starting points', to probe their understanding, to develop new insights into issues and so forth. They are a crucial tool in the classroom, yet often simple things can undermine the quality of what occurs, for example common issues are:

- On average a teacher will wait for between one and three seconds before moving to another pupil if an answer is not forthcoming.
- Poor questions, such as 'guess what is in my head' type questions.
- Teachers often accept a short answer and elaborate on the response themselves.

Table 5.3 provides a more detailed list of potential problems associated with questioning. This table can be usefully employed in a departmental or faculty meeting to explore the issues to do with questioning. Ideally it would be used in conjunction with a suitable video clip or an observation of a colleague, and used to identify strengths or issues when asking questions, before moving on to ways to improve questioning.

Table 5.3 Questioning techniques: what can go wrong?

Below are some common 'errors' that often occur when questioning.
■ Asking too many questions at once.
■ Asking a question and answering it yourself.
■ Asking questions only of the brightest or most likeable pupils.
■ Asking a difficult question too early in the sequence of events.
■ Asking irrelevant questions.
■ Always asking questions of the same type (e.g. closed ones).
■ Asking questions in a threatening manner.
■ Not indicating a change in the type of question.
■ Not using probing questions.
■ Not giving pupils time to think.
■ Not correcting wrong answers.
■ Ignoring pupils' answers.
■ Failing to see the implication of pupils' answers.
■ Failing to build on answers.
■ Getting the language level too high or too low.
■ Assuming too much knowledge.
■ Asking 'guess what's in my head' type questions.
■ Asking questions that do not help pupils meet the lesson objectives
Source: adapted from Wragg and Brown (2001).
Put a tick by any error you think you have done. Are there any circumstances in which these 'errors' may be appropriate?
Compare your 'errors' with someone else. How could you avoid some of these in future – draw up a list of things to bear in mind when asking questions.

Practical task 5.3

When you next observe others asking questions the following questions are a good starting point:

* What good practice can you identify which is worth sharing?

* What concerns did you identify?

* In what ways do the issues you identify hinder children's learning of citizenship/history/geography/RE?

* How can you improve your questioning to avoid these issues?

Ways to improve questioning

Obviously all teachers want to ensure that their questioning is effective, but the extent to which this happens does depend on the nature of the problem. Some issues can be simply addressed through 'think time', or more systematic analysis of the humanities subjects and their specific intellectual demands may be required in order to devise better questions. Below are some suggestions for how questioning may be improved and a range of possible activities to support these.

Think time

There are some simple techniques to promote better questioning, for example 'think, pair, share'. The 'think' provides time to consider an answer, 'pair' allows for sharing that answer with a partner and therefore allows thoughts to be developed, and 'share' means the answer can be presented to the rest of the class. It can be done quickly – say ten seconds for 'think', 30 seconds for 'pair' if necessary – but the approach has a number of benefits:

■ Pupils have time to think and develop an answer (even if they 'borrow' their partner's answer!).

■ The teacher can reasonably expect all pupils to have a response and can therefore choose any pupil to answer – this avoids 'hands up' scenarios where pupils may be able to evade being asked a question.

■ This in turn creates an expectation that all pupils have to engage in the process.

■ As pupils are more likely to be able to offer productive answers this can boost self-esteem and confidence.

It would be useful to work with a colleague on this and do a 'before and after' comparison of the impact such an approach has on the ability of pupils to answer questions.

Prompts and probes

A classic mistake is for teachers to obtain a response from a pupil, but restrict what the pupil says and themselves to elaborate on the answer! Clearly it would be valuable for the teacher to ask further questions, and have a ready list of questions to push the pupil's thinking further, but why not have a list of 'prompts and probes' displayed in the classroom and ask pupils to identify the questions that need to be asked to elicit further ideas. Such 'prompts and probes' could include:

- Tell me a little more.
- Explain your thinking further.
- Do you think that fully explains the question?
- How did you work out that answer?
- Is that the only answer/most likely answer?
- What might people say if they wished to disagree with that point?
- Why do you think this question is important?

Again, devising a series of 'prompts and probes' would be a useful departmental or faculty discussion, to raise both awareness of effective questioning and insights into the expectations in the different humanities subjects.

Using more focused questions

Types of questions

It is important to plan the questions you ask to make sure they support your lesson goals, focus pupils' thinking and promote higher-level thinking. For example, the question 'Why did the First World War start?' could lead to very different responses; at the simplest level a teacher may require an answer merely identifying the assassination of Archduke Franz Ferdinand, a causal explanation (which may or may not require reference to sources), or an analysis of competing interpretations. There are different ways of categorising questions and these can be helpful in analysing and developing your practice by ensuring your questions are clearly focused and develop children's historical thinking. In RE, a teacher may pose the question 'Is it ever possible to truly forgive?', which could also elicit a number of responses. These could include a simple 'gut' reaction based upon a student's own experiences, or might draw upon notions of forgiveness from different faiths and cultures and so require some form of sensitive comparison, or draw upon philosophical discussions of the concept of forgiveness – all of these responses are possible but require the teachers to have a clear sense of the type of thinking they wish to develop (see Figure 5.1 for different types of thinking).

Closed and open questions

This is the simplest way to categorise questions. Closed questions obviously require short responses, often in the form of recall or choosing from two alternatives, whereas open questions require more elaboration. Closed questions are considered 'easy' and are therefore frequently directed at the less able. But they are only easy if you know the answer and so can be problematic, whereas most pupils are actually able to offer a reasoned response. Thinking about open questions, though, is not that helpful because the category is too general. Below are different models of questioning that can be explored to generate open questions. Each model has a set of questions that could be asked based around the general question 'Why did the First World War start?' As you read through these, compare the different models and see which you find the most helpful and effective.

Questions to generate contextual knowledge

Harris and Luff (2004) offer a way of approaching questions by considering how to generate contextual knowledge before pupils can consider the main issues. To understand a topic or issue pupils may need questions that focus on the nature of the issue or topic, questions about earlier work, questions for context, and questions to examine impact, significance and so forth – this actually involves a judicious mix of open and closed questions (see Table 5.4).

Table 5.4 Questions to generate contextual knowledge about 'Why did the First World War start?'

Questions about the outbreak of the war	Questions about earlier work	Questions providing further context about the period	Questions to explain the outbreak of the war
Who was assassinated in Sarajevo? When did the war start? What was the Schlieffen Plan? What were the two alliances called and who was in them?	What other wars have we looked at in the past? What factors were you able to identify that led to these wars? In what different ways were we able to explain why these wars started?	Why were countries so keen to form alliances? What was nationalism and why was it so destabilising? What impact did imperialism have on relations between countries?	To what extent were impersonal factors like imperialism to blame for the outbreak of war? How far was any single country responsible for the outbreak of the war? Why did the war start in 1914 and not earlier?

Hierarchy of questions

Bloom's taxonomy is probably the best-known example of a hierarchy of questions which sets out increasingly complex ways of thinking (see Table 5.5). Though useful the hierarchy is not always that straightforward and the complexity of thinking may stem from elsewhere, for example the need to grasp a concept like globalisation or the amount of knowledge that pupils need to possess (the more they know, the more sophisticated the potential response). There is also a danger that knowledge is seen as a low-level form of thinking and therefore the hierarchical approach to questioning is used as a means of differentiation, with 'easy' knowledge questions being directed towards those regarded as 'less able'. For example, if you have ever played the game 'Trivial Pursuit', how many times have you been frustrated by not knowing the answer to a question? Knowledge questions are actually quite threatening to pupils, because they will either know the answer or not. However if you were asked to explain whether you liked the game, that is a different sort of question and in many ways one that everyone with experience of the game can answer. Similarly if you were asked to compare and contrast 'Trivial Pursuit' with the game 'Monopoly', it is a question to which anyone with experience of the games can produce a worthwhile answer. In both cases, these questions require higher-level thinking but are less threatening to pupils as they should all be able to answer as long as they have had experience of these particular games. In one sense knowledge is easy, as long as students have experience of whatever is being discussed, but we must never overestimate what pupils know; the vast majority of pupils I have come across are able to think, but they may lack the necessary knowledge on which to build that thinking. We need to teach pupils the knowledge they need, but not get too bogged down in asking them knowledge questions; rather we want them to use that knowledge in response to more complex questions. Unfortunately the research evidence (see Muijs and Reynolds, 2005) suggests teachers spend too much time asking low-level questions,

Table 5.5 Hierarchy of questions about 'Why did the First World War start?'

Evaluation (to make judgements)	To what extent was the alliance system the main cause of the First World War?
Synthesis (to create new ideas or bring together ideas)	How similar are the causes of the First World War to other wars you have studied?
Analysis (to take information apart)	How could we categorise the causes of the war?
Application (to use information)	Given what you know about Germany up to 1914, why would Germany support Austria-Hungary's attack on Serbia?
Comprehension (to understand information)	(using information in a table/textbook) Which alliance was the strongest militarily?
Knowledge (to find or remember information)	Who was assassinated at Sarajevo in June 1914? Which countries belonged in which alliance?

Questions that focus on different types of thinking

Unlike Bloom, Husbands (1996) (drawing on the work of Morgan and Saxton) suggests that there is no need to consider whether there is a hierarchy of difficulty; rather there is a need to emphasise that there are different types of thinking and that different questions will support these different ways of thinking, for example questions that elicit information, reflection and understanding (see Table 5.6). This model of questioning is attractive and fits in easily with the discussion above about defining precise learning objectives. It has a mix of closed and open questions, and Table 5.7 shows how this model could be applied to questions about the outbreak of the First World War.

Table 5.6 Questions for developing different types of thinking

Questions which elicit information	Questions which elicit reflection	Questions which elicit understanding	
		Divergent (seeks alternative answers)	Convergent (seeks best answer)
Focus is on recall, recognition, observation	Focus on personal response, may require evaluation, justification, defence of opinion	Focus is on range of possible answers, requiring imagination, hypothesising, inferring	Focus is on what is known and appropriate explanations, interpretations, causal relationships
What is it? Where is it? When did it happen? Who won?	How far was … justified? Do you agree with …? Was this the best way to …?	Given what we know about … why did they do …? Why is it so difficult to find out about …? Which source best tells us about …?	Why did … happen? From the evidence, what can we be sure of? How come there are such different interpretations about …?

Source: adapted from Chris Husbands (1996) *What is History Teaching?* (Buckingham: Open University Press).

Table 5.7 Questions that focus on different types of historical thinking about 'Why did the First World War start?'

Questions which elicit information	Questions which elicit reflection	Questions which elicit understanding	
		Divergent (seeks alternative answers)	Convergent (seeks best answer)
Focus is on recall, recognition, observation	Focus on personal response, may require evaluation, justification, defence of opinion	Focus is on range of possible answers, requiring imagination, hypothesising, inferring	Focus is on what is known and appropriate explanations, interpretations, causal relationships
Who was assassinated in June 1914? What was the main aim of the Schlieffen Plan?	Is it right to argue Germany was responsible for the outbreak of war in 1914? Do you think that war could have been avoided in 1914?	How could we explain why the war started? What is the most important reason why the war started?	Why did the war start? Who was responsible for the outbreak of war?

The questions in Tables 5.4 to 5.7 show how different models of questioning might appear within a subject area, but it is important to think about how you might ask questions that draw upon a cross-curricular approach and so help to deepen pupils' understanding. If we explore the idea of the origins of the First World War, we can see how using the thinking from other subjects can enhance the pupils' understanding of this topic and the outbreak of war in general.

Drawing on geography, pupils might start to explore why the war occurred in Europe, rather than elsewhere; the lead up to the war was characterised by tensions in the Far East, Africa and the Balkans, yet actual conflict started on the borders of France and Germany. A geopolitical understanding of Europe in 1914 can help to explain why the war started as it did. An understanding of place and what it meant to people can also help to explain the growth of nationalist tensions within many of the European states in 1914, whilst an understanding of factors of production, the distribution of resources and related issues can help to explain the economic rivalries that emerged prior to the outbreak of war. Although these are set in a historical context, the geographical ideas of place and space add an extra dimension to pupils' understanding of the causes of the war.

Citizenship may also add a different perspective. Although the First World War is obviously a historical topic, and its origins are particular to the circumstances in 1914, pupils might be asked to speculate more generally as to why wars start; the First World War could be used as a model from which to explore the outbreak of other conflicts. Thus, pupils might explore the extent to which the outbreak of the First World War is typical of wars generally. In addition pupils might explore attempts to prevent the outbreak of the war, and from here explore how wars have been or might in future be averted.

From a RE perspective, pupils could examine the extent to which any war or act of aggression is justifiable, either drawing on the teachings of different religions or drawing upon more philosophical arguments.

Practical task 5.4

If you are a geography, RE or citizenship teacher, take one of your key concepts/processes and/or an area of content and devise a series of questions based around these different models. If you are a history teacher, take another topic and/or concept/process and devise a series of questions. Compare the different questions you identify and evaluate the benefits of these approaches.

Using one of the models above, devise a set of questions around your chosen concept/process/content from the other humanities subjects and see how they could enhance a pupil's understanding of this area.

Compare your questions with those of a subject specialist and discuss any differences between your sets of questions. In this way you may gain further insights into the demands of the range of humanities subjects.

Practical task 5.5

Choose one of the following topics:

* conflict;
* poverty;
* migration;
* crime.

Identify a series of questions (again drawing on one of the models in Tables 5.4 to 5.7) that could be asked that draw upon all four of the humanities subjects.

What do you see as the pros and cons for pupils of such an approach to questioning?

Reflective task 5.1

As an activity, look at the questions asked in Tables 5.4, 5.5 and 5.7 and reflect on the strengths and weaknesses of these different questioning approaches.

Examining these models, which one do you think works best and why? What factors influence your choice of questions (e.g. age of pupils, complexity of topic/concept/process)?

Do some models work better for some subjects than others?

Promoting pupil–pupil talk

Problems with pupil–pupil talk

Talk is seen as being beneficial to learning; it is often when you are forced to articulate thoughts or explain them to others that you develop a deeper understanding of a concept like a sense of place, get to grips with the power of unwitting testimony in sources, or gain deeper insights into identity. Pupils also enjoy the chance to discuss and debate issues (Harris and Haydn, 2006). Yet as Farmer and Knight (1995: 66) point out: 'most classrooms are dominated by teacher talk. Discussion often means little more than question and answer in which, with the best will in the world, often only a few pupils are directly involved.' Even where pupils sit around a table they are often required to work independently of each other and so opportunities for proper group work can be missed.

Pupil–pupil talk may be simply discussing in pairs (in which case something like 'think, pair, share' mentioned above is very useful) or working in larger groups (the optimum group size varies according to the research you read, though most suggest groups larger than five are ineffective; however the group size does depend on the nature and duration of the task). Considering the nature of the task is important if you are trying to promote pupil–pupil talk; for example a project on the transatlantic slave trade or group work to create a presentation on Islamic beliefs could easily become an information trawl, with the only discussion between pupils on the technicalities of how they carry out the work. The task needs to be tightly focused, there needs to be an issue for pupils to grapple with which would benefit from pupils sharing ideas and thoughts rather than simply sharing the workload. A good enquiry question will help, as will appropriate resources to engage pupils in alternative perspectives.

Yet if we want to promote better-quality talk we need, as with most things in teaching, to ensure that pupils are taught how to do what is expected. Nowadays pupils are given a lot of structure to guide their essay writing, and when carrying out research they will be taught research 'skills'. The same approach of support or scaffolding needs to apply to pupil–pupil talk.

There may be much that we can learn from each other. Harris and Ratcliffe (2005) researched the benefits of using 'collapsed days' to teach about socio-scientific issues, where humanities and science teachers worked collaboratively. One of the initial assumptions in the research was that humanities staff would provide the expertise in managing discussion whilst the science staff would provide the specialist content knowledge. However the research suggested that humanities teachers were not that expert at managing pupil discussion, with the notable exception of RE teachers. Given that citizenship education was in its early days at the time the research was carried out, it would be unfair to pass comment on the ability of citizenship teachers to handle discussion lessons, although the nature of citizenship would suggest that this is an area where teachers need to be skilled.

Teachers' use of discussion may well depend on their view of their subject. For example in RE there is a distinction between learning *about* religion and learning *from* religion. An emphasis on the former would imply a greater focus on acquiring knowledge, whereas the latter would require a more open-ended and philosophical approach to learning, which would be difficult to achieve without discussion. Both history and geography could be seen as factual subjects, yet both have the potential to raise important questions which can be debated.

Approaches for developing pupil–pupil talk

Mercer's work (1995, 2000) categorises pupil–pupil talk as cumulative, disputational and exploratory. Cumulative talk is where pupils essentially agree with each other; there is no challenge to ideas and it often reflects a disinterested approach to the topic being discussed. Disputational talk is characterised by argument. However the nature of the talk shows that pupils take entrenched positions and argue vociferously for their view without really giving any consideration to alternative views being expressed. Exploratory talk, though, allows for a full exploration of all ideas before pupils make decisions. It is characterised by a full sharing of ideas, use of questions to ask for clarification/explanation of ideas and careful consideration of a range of possible ideas before a joint conclusion is arrived at. It is a higher quality of talk and has been shown to enhance pupils' attainment significantly. Establishing exploratory talk takes time but can be successfully achieved through a series of activities (see Table 5.8).

Table 5.8 Establishing exploratory talk

Identify the ground rules.
Get pupils to discuss 'good' ways to talk to each other, for example:
- listening carefully;
- staying focused;
- making sure everyone's opinion is heard;
- discussing all the possible ideas;
- asking for explanation of ideas;
- being willing to challenge ideas/open to being challenged;
- respecting other people's views;
- sharing all the information and ideas;
- group taking joint responsibility for decisions reached.

Make sure they practise these rules as they are discussing them!
As a group, then as a class, pupils have to decide which are the most important rules (usually about five or six). Again, make sure they practise what they preach.
Create a class list of ground rules. Refer to these any time exploratory talk activities are used.
There is a useful generic sequence of lessons to establish the ground rules in Dawes et al., *Thinking Together in Geography* (Stevenage: Badger, 2005).

According to some research (Joyce, Calhoun and Hopkins, 1997) pupils need to be organised in four stages to promote better-quality interactions. The stages are: orientation, participant training, operation and debriefing (see Table 5.9).

Table 5.9 Four stages in promoting better-quality interactions

Orientation involves deciding on group selection and size, and classroom layout, as well as explaining the purpose and nature of the task.
Participant training involves allocation of roles (e.g. chair, observer, reporter), clarifying rules and procedures, and practical elements like time frame.
Operation requires monitoring of work, reminders about rules, procedures and purposes of the work, and giving time and encouragement.
Debriefing needs to provide an opportunity for a concrete outcome, a discussion about how well the groups worked together, and a chance for general feedback.

Both Mercer and Joyce, Calhoun and Hopkins offer general approaches to promoting pupil talk, but within these approaches it is helpful to identify specific activities that provide opportunities for pupil–pupil talk.

Activities for promoting pupil–pupil talk

Most classroom tasks could be adapted to promote talk between pupils, as the majority of written tasks that are used could also be carried out orally. Good quality pupil–pupil talk is more likely to arise where it has been planned for, the nature of the topic provokes debate or the type of activity promotes talk. A 2008 article by Haenen and Tuithof in *Teaching History* offers a quick summary of such activities, including: brainstorming, pair work, jigsaw, placemat and word webbing (see Table 5.10 for an outline of these activities.

Table 5.10 'Talk activities' taken from Haenen and Tuithof (2008), by kind permission of The Historical Association

---

Brainstorming
- Form a brainstorming group of at least 4, but no more than 8 pupils
- Briefly think of as many as possible ideas, arguments, examples, associations (opening question: 'What does ... remind you of?')

Be aware of the following brainstorming features:
- Speed, spontaneous thinking, 'who will volunteer, please?'
- Any contribution is a good one; no critical comments on each other's contributions.
- Unusual ideas are also useful; all ideas and suggestions are welcomed.
- Build on each other's contributions in order to expand and add further.

Pair work

Making a written assignment:
Form a group of 4 pupils: A, B, C and D.
- A and B will be working together, as well as C and D.
- A will compare the results with C, as will B with D.
- A and B will then together discuss the differences between the answers, and turn the results into a whole; C and D will do the same.

Making a 'speaking' assignment:
- Form a group of 4 pupils: A, B, C and D.
- A and B discuss the assignment, as well as C and D. Agree on the time they will be allowed (e.g. 3 minutes).
- A and C exchange the discussion results, as do B and D. Agree on a time span.

Jigsaw
The jigsaw is a very useful technique for saving time. Divide the contents (sources, sub-questions, paragraphs) among the pupils. Each member of the group becomes an expert in his/her part and passes his/her knowledge on to the other pupils of the group. Thus, together you will cover and discuss all of the contents of the assignment.

Step 1: Divide the materials or the assignment into equal parts, so that each pupil has a comparable study load.

Step 2: The basic group – Form basic groups in such a way that each group is the size of the number of equal parts; e.g. 4 sub-questions means a group of 4 pupils, numbered 1 to 4.

Step 3: The expert group – All the numbers 1 of the basic groups join together to execute their part of the assignment and become experts in it. The same holds for the numbers 2, 3 and so on.

Step 4: Back to the basic group – The pupils then go back to their basic group to present the results and pass on their knowledge to the other pupils of that basic group. It's important for the teacher to check afterwards whether all of the pupils have indeed become knowledgeable about the subject content.

Placemat
You need a large piece of paper and a felt-tipped pen. Arrange the pupils into groups of four.

- Divide the sheet by drawing 5 separate spaces: four angles and a square in the middle.
- On the outer spaces, each pupil individually and quietly writes down his/her thoughts on the topic.
- Together, the four discuss what each of them has written down, and decide on what are the most important points; these are then written down in the central square by the one of them nominated to do so.
- Each group nominates a spokesman, who then reports the points agreed on to the whole class.

Word webbing
In a group, individually, or with the whole class, make a word web together. When word webbing in a group, you will need a large piece of paper and, for each pupil, a felt-tipped pen with its own particular colour.
- One pupil draws a circle in the middle of the paper and in it writes down the discussion theme.
- Each pupil in turn adds a concept to it.
- If necessary, this round can be repeated in order to add more concepts to the central theme, after which a distinction can be made between the more and the less important concepts.
- Each pupil draws connecting lines between the concepts.
- Eventually, there will be a discussion about the word web; because each pupil used a differently coloured felt-tipped pen, each contribution has been made visible during the process.

Source: from Haenen and Tuithof (2008).

Of course there are a range of other activities that will foster pupil–pupil talk, many of which can be found in the work of Spencer Kagan (1994). Kagan's activities are based around the idea of 'PIES': positive interdependence (P), individual accountability (I), equal participation (E) and simultaneous interaction (S). The aim is to get pupils to work cooperatively because there is a positive group outcome. These activities are clearly not specific to humanities teaching, but are very effective at promoting positive pupil–pupil interaction and talk, and are therefore valuable tools in a teacher's repertoire, because they provoke sharing of ideas, listening to a range of different views and helping pupils to formulate their own opinions, which are open to challenge. Table 5.11 outlines some of these ideas and how they work.

Table 5.11 Activities for promoting pupil–pupil talk

Continuums
Opposing statements are expressed and students have to place themselves along a continuum to indicate their position in relation to the issue. Students can then be challenged to explain their ideas. This activity can be developed further by pairing off pupils who are next to each other in the continuum and can be asked to share their ideas and opinions. The activity can be taken further by then getting pupils (individually or in pairs) to talk to others who have adopted an opposing position on the continuum, and having to share and justify their views.

Corners

This is similar to a continuum but this time students are offered four options in response to an issue, and pupils have to go to a corner that best represents their view. As with the continuum pupils can firstly share their ideas with someone with whom they are in agreement, before going to discuss their views with students in opposing corners.

Team statements

Students are presented with an issue, on which they can reflect individually before having a discussion with a small group. Each member in the group writes down a statement that attempts to sum up the view(s) of the group. The pupils then share these statements within the group, and discuss, challenge and clarify them, before attempting to write one statement which reflects the views of everyone in the group. These can then be shared with the whole class for further discussion.

Paraphrase passport

During discussions, when somebody wishes to speak they have to start by summarising the views and/or ideas of the previous person who has spoken before they can continue – the person whose views have been surmised needs to be happy that their views have been clearly represented before the new speaker can continue. This has the advantage of ensuring students listen to each other carefully, that their views are clarified and are open to challenge.

Numbered heads together

Pupils working in small groups are numbered, e.g. 1–4. A question or issue is presented to the groups in the classroom and the pupils discuss their response in their small groups. The teacher then calls out a number and the pupil in each team with that number has to provide a response, either orally or on a (mini) whiteboard.

Showdown

Students work in small groups, and each member of the group has a mini-whiteboard or sheet of paper. They write down their individual response to a question or issue, and when the teacher or leader in the group calls 'showdown' the group share their responses and discuss their answers.

Silent conversation

This can take many forms, but essentially revolves around a small group of students discussing their initial ideas, e.g. 'what new things have you learnt?', 'what surprises you most about this topic?', 'what questions do you have about the topic?' and so forth, and recording these on a large piece of paper. The next step is carried out in *absolute silence*. Everyone in the classroom gets up, takes a pen or pencil, and moves round to see what other groups have recorded on their sheets of paper. As they read these sheets the students write down comments or questions onto the sheets – it is usually best to provide a limited time frame and to insist that everyone writes at least four things as they move around the room looking at different groups' sheets. At the end of the specified time period, students return to their initial groups, read the comments and questions other students have now written, and discuss these.

Teammates consult

When students have a series of tasks to complete, they start by putting their pens into a pot in the middle of the table, and discuss the first task to be done. Once they are satisfied that everyone in the group understands what must be done or is clear about the answer, the students are allowed to take their pens and complete the task. This is repeated for each subsequent task.

Same–different

Working in pairs, students will have two different pictures or images. They have to identify similarities and differences between the two pictures of images but are not allowed to see each other's picture.

Practical task 5.6

Look at the activities outlined in Tables 5.10 and 5.11.

* Are these activities better suited to particular humanities subjects or are they applicable to all of them?

* Identify a lesson you taught recently.

* Where might you have used one (or more) of these strategies? In what ways might it have enhanced the learning experience of the pupils?

Reflective task 5.2

As an activity you could carry out the following tasks:

* Observe a lesson or watch a suitable video clip. What opportunities were there for pupil–pupil talk? How effective was this pupil–pupil talk? How could the lesson be adapted to accommodate more pupil–pupil talk?

* Identify the barriers to pupil–pupil talk. Look at Tables 5.8 and 5.9, which outline in more detail the approaches of Mercer and of Joyce, Calhoun and Hopkins. How do these ideas overcome the barriers you identified?

* Developing high-quality pupil–pupil talk is a long-term project, which in the short term will be time consuming. What opportunities do you have over a half-term/term/year to develop pupil–pupil talk? What steps do you need to take to develop pupil talk? What activities could you use to develop pupil talk (look at Tables 5.10 and 5.11 for some example activities)?

This chapter has taken a specific focus on talk, not because it is uniquely important to the humanities teacher, but because it is an area that warrants further serious consideration as part of a teacher's pedagogical skills. At the same time, we would argue that learning in the humanities subjects should make extensive use of discussion. The subjects are not just about facts and figures; rather they explore issues that matter in people's lives. Chapter 6 provides a clear indication of this; the chapter deals with controversial and sensitive topics. It would be possible to teach such issues in a straightforward manner from a textbook or series of worksheets, but the topics are full of issues that need to be explored and as such discussion should be a key part of any teacher's pedagogical skills to ensure pupils gain a sound educational experience.

Professional standards for QTS

This chapter will help you meet the following Q standards: Q6, Q7a, Q10, Q12, Q14, Q25c, Q25d, Q28, Q29.

Professional standards for teachers

This chapter will help you meet the following core standards: C6, C7, C15, C29d, C29e, C31, C34.

6

Teaching controversial and sensitive topics

Key objectives

By the end of this chapter, you will have:

- drawn on the methodology outlined in the previous three chapters to explore in detail, through one aspect of the humanities, how teaching controversial and sensitive topics can be addressed through a common methodology that takes advantage of the content and concepts of the humanities subjects;
- addressed the barriers that are perceived to exist;
- explored practical ways in which these barriers can be overcome.

It may seem a little strange that we have decided to give space to a separate chapter on teaching controversial and sensitive topics, as we have generally focused on more generic issues relating to cross-curricular humanities, whereas this area is much more content specific. However the evidence (Historical Association, 2007) suggests that this is an area that creates particular problems for teachers. In addition, given the nature of the humanities and its focus on human thoughts, beliefs and actions, it would be very difficult to avoid teaching topics that deal with people's inhumanity to each other, the injustices that are prevalent in society or the difficulties that are presented in everyday life where tough decisions have to be made. In many ways a cross-curricular approach to the humanities allows students to explore such issues from a range of perspectives and subject angles that will better inform their understanding of these issues and how they can be addressed. A strong case can be made that this is an area where a humanities education is essential and provides a space for all students to engage with issues that are unlikely to occur elsewhere in the curriculum. As the Oxfam (2006) guide 'Teaching controversial issues' makes clear, young people are growing up in a world where there are many issues that are controversial and sensitive, and these students need to explore their own values and perspectives in relation to these issues rather than being sheltered from them. After all, young people will need to address these issues in their own right as they grow into adulthood, so they need opportunities to explore controversial issues in a helpful and supportive environment.

We have also taken the decision to write this chapter in a different way, often using 'I' instead of 'we'. In part this reflects that this area is sensitive; in approaching it, individuals need to make decisions with which they are happy. Also, as one of the authors, Richard Harris, has been involved in a number of initiatives which have affected his own understanding of this area, this chapter reflects a very personal perspective, albeit one which we can all support.

What makes a topic controversial and/or sensitive?

According to the QCA guidance for teaching citizenship (2001: 46), controversial and sensitive topics are defined thus:

> Issues that are likely to be sensitive or controversial are those that have a political, social or personal impact and arouse feeling and/or deal with questions of value or belief.

Oxfam (2006), in their pamphlet on teaching controversial issues, argue that:

> Almost any topic can become controversial if individual groups offer differing explanations about events, what should happen next and how issues should be resolved, or if one side of an issue is presented in a way that raises the emotional response of those who might disagree.

A report produced by the Historical Association (2007: 3) also offered a definition:

> The study of history can be emotive and controversial where there is actual or perceived unfairness to people by another individual or group in the past. This may also be the case where there are disparities between what is taught in school history, family/community histories and other histories. Such issues and disparities create a strong resonance with students in particular educational settings.

All these definitions offer plenty of scope to examine our understanding of such issues. They all indicate that controversy is marked by differing perspectives, although on its own this is not likely to make topics strongly contentious as it will also depend on the nature of the issue being discussed and the strength of feeling being expressed. It is important to recognise that not all topics are controversial or sensitive to all pupils at all times; there is a strong personal element to such issues. Topics that involve injustice are likely to be controversial, but become much more emotive when there is a level of personal involvement.

This was clearly illustrated for me by a trainee history teacher who taught two lessons on whether the UK ought to apologise for its involvement in the transatlantic slave trade. The trainee was able to teach the same lesson in two very different schools. In an essentially white, monocultural setting she witnessed a very interested, but relatively academic, level of debate as pupils weighed up the pros and cons of the different arguments. In her second school placement, in a multi-ethnic school with significant proportions of students from black African and black Caribbean backgrounds, the debate was much more heated and explosive. This is not to say that one response was more desirable than the other, but it is important to recognise that controversial and sensitive topics are very likely to be context specific. Similarly, topics that involve values or beliefs are likely to be controversial, but are especially so where the values and/or beliefs of any particular group are being questioned. Also, as Hopwood (2007) stresses, values that may be promoted could actually be in tension with each other: the desire to protect the environment, for example, may clash with the desire to see economic growth in developing countries to eradicate poverty or to enhance the standard of living in such places.

Whatever definition is accepted, the teaching of controversial and sensitive topics creates particular challenges for teachers. Common concerns raised by teachers include the lack of appropriate subject knowledge, confusion over suitable pedagogical approaches, fears of upsetting or offending pupils and/or parents, being accused of promoting particular standpoints and thereby indoctrinating pupils, and so forth.

The challenge of teaching controversial and sensitive topics

Despite a clear rationale for the role of the humanities subjects in addressing controversial and sensitive topics, the challenges of teaching such topics present a number of obstacles. It is therefore not surprising to discover that there is much evidence which suggests many teachers are not very well equipped to deal with such topics in an effective manner or are simply reluctant to address them.

Kitson and McCully's (2005) study of history teachers in Northern Ireland shows that many teachers are reluctant to address issues that would deal with the troubled past in Ireland. They categorised teachers as avoiders (who would not teach anything controversial) or containers (those who would defuse or cover up the issues), whilst the risk takers (those who did deal with controversial topics) were in a minority. Even where teachers do address challenging topics, this is not always done effectively. Traille's (2006) research highlights the unintended consequences of teaching a unit on 'Black peoples of the Americas', whilst Harris (2010) also highlights the naïve confidence with which teachers might tackle potentially sensitive topics without fully understanding the purpose of teaching such topics, or examining the appropriateness of content and pedagogical approaches.

The section below explores some of the areas teachers should consider more deeply to help them address the teaching of difficult issues. Teachers need to examine what they are hoping to achieve by teaching controversial topics and the values they are trying to promote by doing this. They also need to explore the pedagogical challenges presented by such topics, particularly ideas about balance and neutrality. The section also looks at the emotional 'baggage' related to sensitive topics which pupils bring with them into the classroom.

The issue of values and purpose

Part of the difficulty is for teachers to fully understand what they are trying to achieve when addressing issues that are heavily value laden. According to Klaassen's (2002) study of teachers, the vast majority are very uncomfortable teaching explicit moral values or positions. Partly this is out of a liberal concern that students be allowed to explore and identify their own positions, although as Cotton's (2006) study of geography teachers shows, even where teachers are overtly committed to allowing students to reach their own views, they still find covert ways to impose or support a particular stance they wish pupils to adopt (often without realising this).

One of the key questions teachers need to ask themselves is whether they are simply teaching *about* emotive and controversial issues or teaching students to be able to *do something* about such issues. This distinction was highlighted very starkly on a Council of Europe project entitled 'Education for the prevention of crimes against humanity'. Participants in the project were required to develop materials to address this theme, but it became clear very early on that most materials were *education about* crimes against humanity, often from a historical perspective, as opposed to *education for the prevention* of such acts. This is not to say students should not learn about such events, but the project clearly raised the question for participants about their intended learning goals and the extent to which they felt their role was to examine values and morality explicitly. In this sense it becomes very important to identify the purpose of teaching any given topic. This was revealed very clearly in some recent research (Harris, 2010) which found that trainee teachers who had a clear idea as to why specific topics ought to be taught were more comfortable and confident in their ability to tackle a range of potentially difficult and sensitive topics. This does require, as Nelson (2008) has shown, that fundamental questions are asked, such as what is the point of learning particular topics.

This can be seen in recent debates about the teaching of the Holocaust. Short and Reed (2004) see Holocaust education as a form of anti-racist education, Illingworth (2000) argues for a focus on the moral lessons to be drawn, while Kinloch (2001) believes that the moral lessons to be drawn from the Holocaust are spurious and best ignored. To an extent none of these positions is entirely 'correct'; instead the issue to be considered is: what is the point of teaching a topic as horrific as the Holocaust? For many years this was an issue I faced when teaching the topic in the history classroom. I felt very differently about this topic than about others; in many ways I was awed by the horror of the events and wanted my pupils to experience this and to feel the moral outrage that I did. At the same time however I was aware that my teaching lacked the direction I had identified when teaching other topics. As I became more experienced as a teacher, I began to realise the shortcomings in my approach and focused much more on the importance of addressing stereotypes that often existed in pupils' minds when teaching the Holocaust. I have also come to see that I cannot avoid engaging in discussions about values.

The issues of values is a complicated one, as there is a requirement on teachers not to present one-sided perspectives, plus many teachers would be uncomfortable with the idea that they are somehow 'indoctrinating' pupils to support a particular view. Yet what we do is value laden, because we make choices. As educators we choose what to put in the curriculum, we choose how we want to teach particular topics and so forth. Although our choices may be made for seemingly pragmatic reasons, they are often underscored by values of which we may be unconscious. For example a geography department may well choose to include a include a study on migration with a view to countering stereotypical views that students hold of immigrants; the aim is to promote tolerance and understanding of 'others', which is an important value and one which should probably be overtly pursued.

As part of education it is surely important to support the moral development of young people, which in turn is bound to be shaped by the society in which we live: in our case a society where we adhere to democratic principles and the rule of law. This is not to state that students should be taught to accept particular moral positions unquestioningly, but rather for them to explore the issues underpinning those positions. Kohlberg's (1981) stages of moral development (see Table 6.1) provides one guide to understanding how people justify moral actions, and can shed some light on what teachers are trying to achieve.

Table 6.1 Kohlberg's stages of moral development

Level 1 (Pre-conventional) 1. Obedience and punishment orientation. 2. Self-interest orientation.	At the first stage the emphasis for the individual is to avoid punishment, and this is therefore a very egotistical position, usually found in younger children. At the second stage, actions are governed more by self-interest and what an individual can gain from a situation.
Level 2 (Conventional) 3. Interpersonal accord and conformity (*The good boy/ good girl attitude*). 4. Authority and social-order maintaining orientation.	At this stage, the motivation is to fit in with accepted norms. There is a desire to be liked, achieved by following what is expected. Judgements are often based on understanding what the intended consequences of any actions are. At stage 4 there is a realisation that rules help society function more efficiently and therefore there is a need to uphold these. In one sense this shows individuals realise that the needs of society overrule those of the individual. Additionally people operating at this level feel they have little or no control over what is deemed to be 'good' as this is dictated by society as a whole.
Level 3 (Post-conventional) 5. Social contract orientation. 6. Universal ethical principles.	At this stage, individuals realise that they are separate entities and may hold different principles from those espoused by society. This means that people recognise difference between individuals and groups, which are to be respected. Compromise is seen as a means of mediating tensions caused by differences. Laws are also seen as social contracts rather than as inflexible objects. At the highest level is an understanding that there are universal ethical principles and a commitment to justice; therefore laws which defy these principles are seen as unjust and so should be disobeyed.

Kohlberg's theory has been criticised for emphasising justice at the expense of other values that may provide the basis for moral actions, such as caring; it is seen by some as offering a highly rational explanation for action, whereas moral reasoning may be more intuitive than Kohlberg allows. However it does give an indication of the different positions individuals may adopt when examining controversial issues, and highlights the steps that may be needed to move students towards a more considered idea of their moral positions, although it may not provide a straightforward model of progression. Teachers still need to consider clearly what they are trying to achieve each time they ask students to examine a sensitive or controversial issue.

Hopwood (2007) outlines a useful summary of possible outcomes relating to values, which may help teachers of whatever subject clarify their intentions. Hopwood identifies these as:

■ *Values inculcation* – aimed at getting pupils to adopt a particular view.

■ *Values analysis* – where pupils are asked to assess evidence to support a view or set of views.

■ *Growth of moral reasoning* – where pupils are asked to discuss reasons why particular viewpoints are held.

■ *Values clarification* – aimed at helping pupils identify their own values.

■ *Action learning* – where pupils are encouraged to develop ideas with a view to taking some form of action.

Values inculcation is specifically geared towards overtly shaping a student's views; values analysis and growth of moral reasoning are focused more on exploring the basis of a given view, while values clarification is intended to help students examine their own perspectives and values, with action learning requiring students to do something to put these values into practice. These outcomes can be related to the different levels in Kohlberg's stages of moral development, although probably not in the linear way set out by Kohlberg. For example action learning, where pupils decide to put their values into practice, could be dictated by Kohlberg's 'self-interest orientation', or by the need to maintain social order, or be based on universal ethical principles. It therefore seems important to ensure pupils are introduced to the different forms of moral reasoning and helped to explore the positions they hold, and explore the basis of a range of different perspectives, attitudes and beliefs.

Practical task 6.1

The above section has explored the importance of considering values and purpose. Consider how this might be practically applied to a controversial or sensitive issue you currently teach. Revise your planning of this to ensure pupils are:

* introduced to different forms of moral reasoning;

* helped to explore the positions they hold;

* enabled to explore the basis of a range of different perspectives, attitudes and beliefs.

The issue of balance and neutrality

Apart from understanding the complex issues surrounding values, teachers also have to understand the debates about the different ways they could approach the teaching of sensitive issues. Broadly speaking there are three main positions that could be adopted: neutral chair, where the teacher states no position and ensures all sides of an issue are debated; committed stance, where the views of the teacher are expressed at the outset of the debate; and devil's advocate, where the teacher argues for alternative views to those expressed by pupils. Of these three, the stated commitment is one with which many teachers are uncomfortable (for reasons explained above, as it requires teachers to adopt an overt moral position); moreover, stating a commitment to a position is likely to stifle debate amongst students unwilling to challenge the authority of the teacher.

Consequently there is much support for the neutral chair and devil's advocate approaches, both in the literature and in teachers' practice. Wellington (1988: 6) claims that: 'Pupils should be helped to approach controversy not with the expectation that authority figures can resolve issues for them but with a recognition of their right to arrive at their own judgement.' This would suppose that teachers adopt a balanced approach towards teaching controversial issues. They would either have to adopt the stance of a neutral chair and encourage a range of alternative views to be expressed, or move into the role of devil's advocate to ensure alternative views were presented that would otherwise be ignored. When confronted with topics that are sensitive, the natural reaction of many teachers is to adopt a balanced approach when teaching. Thus a number of trainee history teachers, when interviewed about their views on teaching a range of diverse topics, often mentioned the need to look at both sides of an issue; for example, when teaching about the British Empire, many felt the positive and negative aspects of the topic should be presented to pupils for them to draw their own conclusions (see Harris, 2010).

Yet each of these positions presents their own dilemmas. Cotton's (2006) study of three geography teachers showed that each wished to adopt a balanced or neutral position when teaching about controversial environmental issues. Cotton highlights how the teachers used strategies to elicit students' views, allowed them to discuss their views and challenged these views to explore alternatives. Yet in practice it proved to be impossible for the teachers to adhere to their stated goal of balance and/or neutrality. Through the use of questioning (particularly in terms of which views were challenged through these questions), the selection of students to answer questions, the use of rhetorical questions, or teachers answering their own questions, the teachers (unconsciously in most cases) were able to control the discussions and promote their own particular slant on the issues. As Cotton concludes (2006: 237):

> all of the teachers studied experienced great difficulty in implementing their beliefs about balance and neutrality, and the classroom data suggest that the influence of the teachers' own environmental attitudes was greater than they either intended or, in all probability, realized.

The problem of neutrality is highlighted by Short and Reed (2004), particularly in respect to the Holocaust. Neutrality on the part of the teacher may be regarded 'as an inability to decide where truth and justice lie with regard to Nazi racial ideology' (Short and Reed, 2004: 53) and may also be interpreted as indifference and so the topic is seen as unimportant. Further, Kitson (2007a, 2007b) shows that attempts to be even-handed in the presentation of views can dehumanise the past and fail to engage pupils with the events.

The idea of adopting a balanced approach has additional difficulties. Banks (2006) makes the point that balance presumes some form of neutral mid-point that can be identified. He argues that balance is an issue of power and raises the questions 'What is balance?' and 'Who decides?' What may be identified as a mid-point by one person may easily be disputed by another. As well, the selection of material to create a balanced perspective may itself skew how a topic is seen. For example there is some dispute about the impact of humans on climate change, yet the overwhelming perspective is that human action has had a negative effect on climate; what might this look like in terms of a 'balanced' approach in the classroom? Should the teacher offer an equal number of resources from each side or offer more materials that argue about the negative impact; the danger here is that students judge a topic by how much evidence they are presented with, rather than assessing the value of the evidence presented. This becomes trickier when examining disputes that involve much more personal and/or emotive issues. Ultimately this suggests it is impossible to present any truly balanced picture of events, which implies we need to take a different approach towards the idea of 'balance'.

One possible approach is offered in a European project, which is part of a wider project known as the Pestalozzi programme (run by the Council of Europe). One of the overriding aims of this programme is to promote democratic citizenship and values, and respect for others. The programme advocates the use of multiple perspectives. The distinction between this and a 'balanced' approach is subtle but important. A multiple-perspective approach obviously explores different views regarding a topic (and could therefore be seen as 'balanced') but it does not assume there is a 'mid-point' or centre ground. Instead it affirms that there are competing views that have validity from different people's perspectives and that it is important for these to be recognised but also evaluated. This provides a means for teachers to approach such topics more confidently, although it still leaves open the question about whether teachers wish to promote an overt moral agenda.

Another issue related to balance is linked to textbooks. Many school textbooks are written with an authoritative voice and appear to present a reasonable and even-handed approach to topics, but they often reflect stereotypes or may unintentionally misrepresent views of people, places or events. This can be seen in the selection of content included in a textbook and the use of images. Many teachers are unaware of the limitations of textbooks, as understandably they may not be experts in all areas of the curriculum. It is therefore important that teachers take steps to improve their subject knowledge to counteract the shortcomings in many textbooks. This is not to say that textbooks should be avoided, but rather their limitations can be used as a teaching technique and pupils can be challenged to 'beat the textbook' by producing more informed pieces of text or more carefully selected choices of images that represent a multiple-perspective approach.

Reflective task 6.1

Where in your own subject knowledge do gaps exist that lead to sole reliance on a textbook? What steps can you take to broaden your subject knowledge in these areas? Having done so, how does this alter your use of this textbook and, more importantly, your pupils' use of it?

Identify topics where you have tried to adopt a 'balanced' approach. How might your teaching of this topic differ if you adopted a 'multiple-perspective' approach instead?

The issue of 'emotional baggage'

One of the concerns that teachers mention when dealing with sensitive content is how pupils will respond. This issue is even more acute when pupils have a personal interest in the topic being examined and therefore have a degree of 'emotional baggage'. This again presents teachers with a dilemma. As mentioned by Kitson (2007a, 2007b), attempts to defuse such topics can make them bland and anodyne, therefore failing to capitalise on pupils' vested interest in a topic. There is great value therefore in building on pupils' innate interest. At the same time however, engaging with pupils' personal interests can lead to fiery disputes in classrooms where pupils promote their entrenched views without listening seriously to the views of others. To an extent the suggestions for promoting talk discussed in Chapter 5 can address this, particularly the emphasis on exploratory talk. Another method which has been used involves the use of distancing techniques. This essentially involves the use of fictional characters that nonetheless represent genuine partisan views (see McCully and Pilgrim, 2004). In such exercises it is important at the outset for students to recognise their deeply held views; exercises that explore stereotypes can be useful in highlighting these. Examples might be a series of statements that pupils have to agree/disagree with, or asking pupils to draw a picture that represents their understanding of a person/event. Clearly, debriefing of pupils' perspectives and alternative perspectives needs to be done explicitly so that pupils understand their own perspectives and can start to understand where their views and those of others come from.

Reflective task 6.2

To what degree can pupils' personal interest be anticipated and planned for? How much of the issue of 'emotional baggage' can be dealt with through specific planning within a lesson? And how much needs to be addressed through a long-term cross-curricular development of pupils' disposition towards engaging constructively with this?

Planning to teach controversial and sensitive topics

Following on from the section above, there are a number of questions that need to be asked when teaching controversial and sensitive topics. The answers to these questions do often overlap, and the answers to some questions are contingent upon the answers to other questions, but collectively they provide a means of examining what is needed for a successful cross-curricular approach to teaching difficult topics.

- What topics should be taught, and what specific content ought to be covered and why?
- What should be the outcome(s) of teaching these topics?
- What are the advantages of adopting a cross-curricular approach to teaching these topics? What do the different humanities subjects bring to these topics?
- What issues, misconceptions and/or stereotypes are pupils likely to have which need to be examined?
- What 'emotional baggage' are pupils likely to bring with them?
- What pedagogical approaches are likely to be most effective in helping pupils develop a deeper understanding of these topics?

Let us explore one possible topic that is already frequently taught, namely the Holocaust, and follow through with the questions posed above. Although it is a commonly taught topic, particularly in history and RE, the topic is often approached in isolation by these subject teachers, who are therefore missing opportunities to support each other and deepen pupils' understanding. When I was teaching we often found that students had already come across the Holocaust in RE previously and that we were 'retreading' some ground, as well as having to address some errors in our colleagues' historical context. In addition I often wondered what we did differently as a history department compared with the RE department. This question continues to puzzle me, having taken groups of history and RE PGCE students on numerous occasions to the Imperial War Museum to learn about teaching the Holocaust. Frequently the history and RE trainees have a limited understanding of what the other subjects do and therefore what they can contribute to the study of the Holocaust; often RE trainee teachers think history just teaches what happened and completely ignores any moral questions, whereas history trainees often believe RE only looks at the features of Judaism and asks the question 'Where was God?' – I appreciate this does an injustice to many students with a more nuanced understanding, but this often reflects the starting point of trainee teachers before they learn to appreciate the value of each other's subjects. How much easier and more productive would it have been, and be, for us to communicate!

So what are the issues that need to be considered before we can ensure a fruitful level of subject collaboration?

What topics should be taught, what specific content ought to be covered and why?

The topic here is clearly the Holocaust and it is included in the curriculum because it is a significant event in human history, but the actual content that ought to be covered is potentially extensive. It is easy to limit the content to the events of Nazi Germany, so covering the period 1933–1945 and the actions taken against the Jewish population of Europe. Immediately there are two issues to consider. Firstly, should the period be limited to 1933–1945 and secondly, should the Holocaust be broadened to include all the groups persecuted by the Nazi regime? In both cases I would argue that the scope needs to be broadened. Although the Holocaust is a specific event linked to the Nazi regime, limiting the topic to the period 1933–1945 ignores a longer history of Jewish persecution, which is not simply an issue confined to Germany. This would also limit the ability to appreciate Jewish culture and life before 1933, so Jewish life only becomes understood in the context of the Holocaust, which is likely to create unhelpful stereotypes. Secondly, although there are disputes about the precise definition of the Holocaust (and whether the term can only be applied to Jewish victims of the Nazi regime), persecution was widespread and so other victims of the period need to be recognised. This in turn raises further questions about the topic being studied – should it be broadened to encompass persecution more generally or focus on genocide? In both cases the Holocaust becomes an example of persecution and/or genocide, implying that additional examples should be taught.

Even if teaching were restricted to the Holocaust and what happened to the Jews, this raises further questions about what content to include. For example, should the focus be on what happened and why it happened, or should it include examples of Jewish resistance and help offered by non-Jews, or focus on the role of the bystander? Should specific individual case studies be included (and if so which ones and why) or should the full scale of the tragedy be examined? As you can see the choice of content is not straightforward. To a large extent the answers will depend on the responses to the other questions, but at this stage these issues need to be raised to help think through the other questions.

What should be the outcome(s) of teaching these topics?

As discussed earlier in this chapter, the question of teaching values is a complicated one, and there have been disputes as to the purpose of teaching the Holocaust per se, so there is scope for a range of possible outcomes. What I would stress here however is the need to ensure a match between content and outcomes. Although this may sound obvious I have often seen lessons where the choice of content does not allow teachers to fully achieve their goals. It is very easy to choose content without fully thinking through the implications of those choices.

To me, students need to understand how people can treat each other (both positively and negatively), the mechanisms by which this can happen and therefore the potential for preventing future occurrences of oppression. In some ways the Holocaust represents a breakdown in human thought and action. For the majority of people there was a breakdown between ideas, beliefs, attitudes and actions. It is easy for people to object to or be horrified by acts of violence but at the same time to feel helpless in the face of the power of the state and therefore do nothing – thus creating a disconnection between beliefs and attitudes on the one hand and actions on the other. However we surely want to teach students that they are not helpless, that they can influence what happens and that collectively people can make things happen, even in the face of threats.

If this is the case, then it starts to make it easier to identify possible content. Context needs to be provided, through study either of persecution generally or of genocide, so that the Holocaust is not seen as a unique aberration, as this implies it is unrepeatable and the power of the lessons to be learnt are therefore diminished. The study of the Holocaust needs to be humanised, so that students appreciate that the people caught up in it were complex individuals who lived real lives, so as to avoid simplistic generalisations about victims, perpetrators and bystanders. This helps to make the topic seem more 'real' and pertinent to people's lives today. This suggests the power of individual stories need to be utilised. Students need to understand how and why such things can happen, they need to examine the choices and dilemmas of those caught up in the events and thereby start to explore how they might react given such extreme circumstances; such a study may raise 'difficult' and uncomfortable knowledge as students explore what they would really do as opposed to what they think they would do.

Clearly these are not the only possible outcomes from a study of the Holocaust but they help to give shape to the overall process of decision making explained here, and hopefully offer some idea as to the process involved.

What are the advantages of adopting a cross-curricular approach to teaching these topics? What do the different humanities subjects bring to these topics?

A cross-curricular approach to a topic such as the Holocaust has many advantages. Not least it allows a variety of learning outcomes to be addressed which may not rest easily within a single subject. For example history readily provides a context as to what happened and how it happened, gives insights into why it happened, and can be used to provide a longer historical perspective by examining persecution at other points in time. Yet history teachers may feel more uncomfortable with directly addressing issues of values and morality, whereas these are areas with which RE teachers are much more familiar. RE teachers may wish to focus on aspects of Judaism and develop an understanding of the Jewish faith as well, although it is not recommended that the Holocaust falls within a specific unit on Judaism, because that has the potential to generate unhelpful stereotypes by linking Judaism with mass slaughter. It may well be better for RE teachers to take the theme of persecution and to explore the issues associated with that. An alternative may be to explore a concept like forgiveness or atonement, either set as part of a broader enquiry, such as 'how far is it possible to truly forgive someone?', or made specific to the Holocaust and asking 'is it possible to forgive people for atrocities committed during the Holocaust?'. Either approach would provide an engaging, complex and challenging perspective on the topic.

A citizenship perspective would bring the issues into the contemporary world and so immediately address any concern about seeing the Holocaust as a 'one-off' unrepeatable event. The Holocaust raises all sorts of questions about the role of the state, the rights and actions of individuals within the state, the role of the international community in preventing future acts of violence against groups, issues of punishment and culpability and so forth.

Although the links between the Holocaust and geography may not be immediately apparent to those outside the subject, Lambert (2004) argues for the importance of understanding that events such as the Holocaust occur within a geographical space. This added dimension can help to deepen a student's understanding of such events. As Lambert explains, geographical concepts helped to inform the ideas of the Nazi regime; the development of geopolitics changed Europe from 'a "blank canvas" to an ideologically charged landscape occupied by people with differentiated rights to citizenship of an *exclusive* sort because it was based on racial grounds' (Lambert, 2004: 45). In this sense geographical thinking adds to the historic context. Geography also helps to explain the spatial element of the Holocaust; the location of the concentration camps and their satellite camps, as well as the death camps, was dictated to an extent by the existing infrastructure of railways and the need for isolated areas. Lambert (2004) and Moss (n.d.) also argue that an understanding of place and identity helps to explain the Holocaust; as Lambert (2004: 46) explains, 'It is even possible to understand the rightness ordinary citizens felt of their actions when their understanding of people and places (the stuff of human geography) has been shaped and distorted by the products of *Ostforschung*.'[1]

Cutting across all the subjects are other themes such as identity. For example, what did it mean to be Jewish at the time and what does it mean now, what did it mean to be German then and what does it mean now, and how should we as individuals see ourselves in relation to 'others'? These are all important questions about humanity and only by exploring controversial and sensitive topics from a range of subject perspectives can we realistically support students' developing understanding of themselves and their place within the world.

What issues, misconceptions and/or stereotypes are pupils likely to have which need to be examined?

It is accepted now that students are not 'empty vessels' waiting to be filled with knowledge, but equally we must not assume that pupils know a great deal about any topic they are taught. There is a need then to examine what pupils know about a topic and to use this as a means of understanding their preconceptions.

The excellent 'Reflections' pack produced by the Imperial War Museum has an interesting range of activities designed to do this, one of which involves exploring stereotypes of what students understand by victims, rescuers and perpetrators, before students are asked to identify what they already know about the Holocaust. What generally emerges from such an exercise is the idea that poor, helpless Jews were murdered by evil, merciless Germans and occasionally rescued by a heroic figure.

Such an exercise helps to identify the need to show that there was not a uniform Jewish experience and not all were victims, and that Jews were not the only victims of Nazi persecution and atrocities. To avoid the issue of 'victimhood', those affected need to be 'humanised', so their culture and lifestyle before the Holocaust needs to be examined. Clearly students need to distinguish between the German people and the Nazi political regime and ideology, and also to see German history in a broader context and not merely focus on the period 1933–1945. Similarly, so-called rescuers are not simple characters who uniformly do good as a matter of course, nor are they all typically heroic figures.

The value of identifying such pupil pre/misconceptions is that it opens up interesting and fruitful avenues for teaching. It helps to identify issues and challenges that students will find engaging as their ideas are questioned and they are required make new meaning.

What 'emotional baggage' are pupils likely to bring with them?

To a large extent this will depend very much on the context in which you teach. Not all topics are controversial and sensitive to all pupils. Although the Holocaust may be a sensitive topic, particularly to those of Jewish descent or related to others embroiled in the events, it is not necessarily controversial unless pupils have a view that it did not happen or that somehow what happened was 'deserved'. Teachers are best placed to make decisions about this based upon their understanding of their own context; however, this should not be used as an excuse to avoid a topic but rather to help teachers look at ways to teach the topic – as a trainee teacher of mine explained: 'you don't look at a class and think "I am not going to do this with them"; rather you look at a class and think "how am I going to do this with them?"'. For example, Alison Stephen (2005), who teaches in a school with a significant Muslim pupil population, had to find ways to help these students understand the Arab–Israeli conflict from both a Muslim and a Jewish perspective. Through a careful use of contextualisation of the events and a focus on the importance of place, she was able to do this effectively and get pupils to look at events from different groups' perspectives. The use of distancing techniques as mentioned above would need to be considered.

What pedagogical approaches are likely to be most effective in helping pupils develop a deeper understanding of these topics?

Whatever the context however, teachers need to think carefully about how they present the topic so as not to traumatise or desensitise students to the issues. One obvious point concerns the use of images, particularly graphic images of violence or destruction. The purpose of such images can only be to shock students by highlighting the barbarity of what took place, yet there are other ways to help students appreciate this without showing them degrading images of other human beings (which in turn can only make them appear more inhuman). The use of artefacts is one way, although this depends upon access to such materials or museums. Alternatives include the use of personal stories; my PGCE students and I have found the book *Erika's Story* to be a remarkably powerful way to engage pupils and to raise a whole host of issues and questions. Again the Imperial War Museum's 'Reflections' pack is a valuable source of ideas and materials.

Obviously the approaches chosen need to be in line with your intended outcomes and selection of content. If your intention is to address stereotypes, then it is important to look at contextualising the Holocaust by exploring the lives of those who were persecuted before 1933 and/or provide an outline of the history of Germany, and the broader history of the persecution of the Jewish people. Both can be achieved through timelines, use of 'little stories', and map work to provide a spatial element to the diversity of experience. Sarah Herrity, a history AST in Hampshire, has devised a very interesting enquiry around the persecution of Jews in medieval Southampton deliberately to debunk the stereotypes that many students bring with them into the classroom. Time can be devoted to the culture and beliefs of those involved.

To explore the dilemmas of those involved requires decision-making exercises and possibly role-play scenarios. To follow up on the relevance of the issues nowadays requires further decision making and problem solving exercises, as well as getting pupils to reflect upon their own attitudes, beliefs and actions. All of these approaches will require students to be adept at discussion and debate (as outlined in Chapter 5).

As can be seen, teaching emotive and controversial topics is not easy and requires a great deal of thought and careful preparation. That is not an excuse, however, for not addressing such topics. These topics help young people understand much about what it means to be human and how humans relate to each other in society, and in humanities subjects this should be the 'bread and butter' of what is included in our curricula. It is clearly important for young people to have such opportunities to explore these topics and the issues that arise in an educational context so as to help them explore their own perspectives and values, and to understand better what has happened, why, and what needs to be done in future. These perspectives cannot be explored by any one subject in isolation, which is why it is important to appreciate the benefits of drawing upon knowledge, concepts and processes from the range of humanities subjects.

Reflective task 6.3

Consider your existing curriculum. How many opportunities are there for pupils to explore controversial issues in depth? What do you feel pupils have to gain from a study of controversial issues? What challenges do such topics present for you as a teacher?

Take another topic and work through the questions outlined above, to develop a cross-curricular approach to another controversial and sensitive topic.

To sum up, controversial and sensitive topics present particular challenges, which often means that teachers either avoid teaching them or do not do them justice. In many ways this is understandable, but there are many benefits for pupils from a focus on such topics, not least the realisation that the humanities subjects are highly relevant and central to any understanding of humanity and the world in which we live.

Professional standards for QTS

This chapter will help you meet the following Q standards: Q6, Q7a, Q8, Q14, Q18, Q19, Q25a, Q30.

Professional standards for teachers

This chapter will help you meet the following core standards: C6, C7, C8, C15, C18, C19, C29a, C37a.

Note

1. *Ostforschung*, meaning 'research on the East', was used in the 1920s supposedly to demonstrate that Germans had historical, sociological, racial and linguistic grounds upon which to claim large areas of central and eastern Europe.

7

Assessment and progression within the humanities

Key objectives

By the end of this chapter, you will have:

- considered some of the different purposes of assessment;

- examined what good practice in assessment is in general terms and more specifically with regard to humanities subjects;

- explored why a clear understanding of good practice in assessment should inform the construction of cross-curricular work;

- reflected upon the implications for assessment of taking a competency-based approach to the curriculum;

- considered what progression could be like in the humanities subjects;

- reflected upon the implications of planning for progression and assessment when considering taking a more integrated approach to the curriculum.

This chapter will promote the view that the processes of assessment and progression are vital parts of curriculum development. Through case studies we will demonstrate just how challenging yet crucial it is for teachers to think in terms of assessment and progression in their own particular subject areas before we can truly think about how to apply this using a more cross-curricular approach. We will also consider how the use of National Curriculum level descriptors has impacted upon teachers' understanding of these two processes. Finally we will think through the implications of planning for assessment and progression in humanities subjects when considering taking a more cross-curricular approach.

> ## Reflective task 7.1
> ## Why do we assess students?
>
> It is best if you work with another colleague on this task, either from your department or, better still, with someone who teaches a different humanities subject from you.
>
> Place your hand in the middle of a blank piece of paper and draw around it. This will give you a hand shape on the page. On your own, come up with your five main reasons why assessment is so important for pupils, teachers, parents and schools. Write each one on a different finger of your paper version of your hand. Once you have your five fingertip reasons:
>
> 1. Check to see if you agree with your colleagues.
> 2. Discuss which of the agreed reasons you think the school seems to value the most.
> 3. Discuss which reason you think best helps the pupils improve the most.
> 4. Which reason best helps you as a teacher?
> 5. Are your answers to question 2 the same as the answers to question 3 and 4? We would be surprised if they were – but why are they different?

It is fair to say that in the first few years of the twenty-first century schools have become obsessed with assessment. There are few schools in the country which do not have a clear assessment policy, a data manager and enough assessment information to fill a number of computers' entire hard drives. This point was highlighted recently by one of the authors' conversation with a maths colleague who has been teaching since the mid-1980s. Like any good archivist the said Maths teacher has kept every mark book he has created since he started teaching in 1985. He was amazed when he chanced to compare a 1980s version with the latest addition to his collection. He said there was more data in his most recent book *by December* than he had in an entire year in the 1980s. His early version was much more concerned with attendance than measuring progress. Does his early mark book suggest there was a lack of assessment policies in place in this one particular school? Or does it perhaps highlight the fact that teachers are being forced to spend far more time assessing students' work today? Or could it show that he spent his early career teaching without even thinking about assessment? We could go on and argue about the reasons for the difference between the inputs in the two mark books ad infinitum. The fact remains that we assess students today more than ever, and record these findings more than ever too. This was recognised as far back as 1993 by Gipps and Stobbart, who stated that students 'going through compulsory education in England and Wales will be the most assessed the education system has ever produced'.

If we return here to the preliminary reflective task, were your findings the same as ours? The five reasons why we assess could be seen to be:

1.   To record how well students are doing.

2.   To report how well students are doing.

3.   To use data to compare and evaluate how well students are doing compared to each other – and therefore how well schools are doing in comparison.

4.   To identify how well students are doing – that is, what they do well and where they need to improve – and to share this with the students.

5.   To help teachers plan the next stages of learning by taking into account what the students have done well and what they need to do to improve.

The above five reasons are not etched in stone as the five 'must' reasons for assessment. But they are a good starting point. In discussions that we have had with numerous teachers at recent in-service training events, it seems that the reasons for assessment that the teachers think schools value most are recording, reporting and using data to compare how well students are doing. In contrast, the reasons which teachers think help students improve the most, and the reasons which help teachers help students the most, are identifying strengths and areas for improvement, sharing this with the students, and using this information to plan the next stages of learning. Surely, if schools are truly institutions that value assessment as a vehicle for improvement then they should place more emphasis on using assessment to help students improve, rather than using assessment to record, report and compare student progress. Don't get us wrong, there has been a great deal of outstanding work done in recent years under the heading 'Assessment for learning', pump primed by Black and William (1998), and the New Labour government encouraged schools to adapt these approaches. But have they really filtered down the classroom of the humanities teacher?

What is good assessment practice?

Before we can consider what effective cross-curricular assessment practice looks like, we need to explore what good assessment practice actually is. There appears to be widespread agreement that effective assessment should aim at promoting good learning. It is not our intention to argue that summative assessment has no place in schools. Indeed, summative assessment data is important for many reasons, as a tool to measure whole-school, departmental and student improvement. It can also be used by classroom teachers to promote useful discussions with their pupils in order to interpret what the summative marks and grades mean for them (Savage, 2011). So what is good assessment? In 2008 the QCA published the updated version of the National Curriculum. It gave the following key principles with regard to assessment:

- The learner is at the heart of assessment.

- Assessment needs to provide a view of the whole learner.

- Assessment is integral to teaching and learning.

- Assessment includes reliable judgements about how learners are doing related, where appropriate, to national standards.

We would not argue with these general principles. Indeed when trying to work in a cross-curricular way this is sound advice. It also agrees with specific advice given to humanities teachers. Haydn, Arthur and Hunt (1997: 208) noted that:

> if assessment is to be used successfully by the classroom teacher it must be integrated within the whole process of planning. … Consequently the way in which you provide feedback to your pupils and both record and report on their progress will be very much related to the clarity of your teaching and learning objectives, together with your choice of learning experiences.

Weedon and Butt (2009) have advised geography teachers that they 'need to have a clear idea about how assessment, teaching and learning interact so [they] can help pupils acquire and develop geographical capability while using the specialised *vocabulary* of geography meaningfully'. Clearly, good assessment should not be an afterthought or bolt-on. It really should be part of the planning process and informed by the teaching and learning. Ofsted (2003: 3) have wholeheartedly supported this view:

> Where assessment is effective in history:
> Assessment activity permeates the work, including planning, teaching, assessing through a range of modes, and evaluating on the basis of assessment information.

There is further agreement in general advice offered to teachers to sum up what good assessment practice looks like. Scott-Baumann, Bloomfield and Roughton (1997: 127), cited in Phillips (2002), explain what effective assessment is. They suggested that assessment should be:

- meaningful and clear to understand by teachers, pupils and parents;
- conveyed in language that is accessible to pupils;
- based on a variety of modes and approaches;
- consistent and reliable as far as it can possibly be;
- organised in order to identify pupils' strengths as well as weaknesses, and how to resolve these weaknesses in order to improve achievement and performance;
- used to inform planning of teaching but not to dominate it;
- designed using good examples that pupils can draw upon and improve.

Thompson (2009) gives ten similar key principles for teacher assessment:

- It should flow from the main teaching and learning activities pupils have been engaged in, not be something tagged on at the end of an arbitrary period.
- It needs to be planned across the key stage.
- It needs to be standardised across the department and applied consistently in all year groups.
- It needs to look at all elements of pupils' achievement.
- It must allow pupils of all abilities to show what they can do.

- It must not rely solely on written outcomes and should use well-chosen stimulus material.

- It must be simple to record the outcomes, neither too blunt an instrument nor spuriously precise. So, there should be no use of level descriptors on individual pieces of work and no decimalised sub-levels.

- It must yield examples of work which can then be moderated then annotated and referred to in a portfolio.

- It must be susceptible to self and peer assessment, by making the mark schemes pupil friendly.

- It must provide help to pupils on how to improve. It must be formative.

It is therefore clear that there is much agreement about what constitutes good assessment practice for humanities teachers. In summary, assessment should be integral to teaching and learning; it should be diagnostic; it should show students the strengths and weaknesses of their work so they can improve; it should inform teachers on the next stages needed in their planning, and no one type of assessment should dominate. Indeed Thompson (2009) stated that, 'We just need a mixed economy and need to be aware of the shortcomings of over mining in one particular area.' He is of course alluding to the over-use of National Curriculum level descriptors to mark individual work and give feedback.

The problem of the National Curriculum level descriptors

Here, unfortunately there is a problem. A strong consensus exists on how to use the National Curriculum level descriptors for assessment amongst researchers, academics and even Ofsted. In nearly all schools, this advice is simply being ignored. One type of assessment does seem to be dominant when it comes to whole-school assessment data: the end-of-half-term 'levelled' piece. If we are to take a cross-curricular approach to planning and teaching we really do need to be mindful of this, especially if we are required to report on 'levels' of progress at intermittent points of KS3. Exactly who makes this judgement and how do they do so in a cross-curricular scheme of work or a more integrated curriculum? Making such a judgement is a skilled job. Teachers of RE and citizenship, until the 2008 National Curriculum, did not have end of key stage levels to refer to, and therefore before 2008 teachers could not decide on a best-fit level for their students. However, they do now. RE and citizenship teachers really should speak to their humanities colleagues and learn from the difficulties encountered by history and geography since 1991, and from the best practice that has developed since then.

Let us remind ourselves how we should be using the National Curriculum level descriptors in the humanities subjects. A strong consensus exists on how to use the National Curriculum level descriptors for assessment in the humanities subjects amongst researchers, academics and even Ofsted. Writing for the Geographical Association, Hopkin (2006: 1) stated:

Level descriptions were intended to be used for long-term assessment, to help teachers reach a rounded judgement of pupils' attainments at the end of a Key Stage. They were designed to be used as 'best fit' descriptions to come to an overall judgement, drawing together evidence of what pupils know, understand and can do in relation to the taught curriculum. ... The level descriptions were not designed to be used as if they were assessment objectives, nor to be broken down into different elements; they were never intended to be used as instruments to assess individual exams, tests, homework or class based exercises.

Phillips (2002) wholeheartedly supported this. He said that by the end of a term or year or key stage, teachers should have built up the knowledge and evidence about pupil performance:

across a range of work, and in a variety of contexts to enable judgements to be made in relation to the level descriptions; this is referred to as a 'rounded judgement' which:

- is based on your knowledge of how pupils perform across a range of contexts;
- takes into account different strengths and weaknesses of the pupils' performance;
- is checked against adjacent level descriptor to ensure that the level awarded is the closest overall match to the pupils' performance in the attainment target.

Burnham and Brown (2004: 5) totally agree. Writing in the HA journal *Teaching History* they state: 'The National Curriculum level descriptions are designed as "best fit" statements to be used only at the end of the Key Stage. ... They are not designed to be used on a half-termly basis throughout the Key Stage and certainly not for single pieces of work.' Ofsted also agrees. The 2011 Ofsted report *Geography: Learning to make a world of difference* reported that,

Many of the departments were being required to sub-divide the levels of the National Curriculum to identify clearly how students were making progress. This was not, however, how level descriptions were intended to be used. In addition, the sub-levels were often an unreliable indicator of how a student was progressing, since progress could vary across different aspects of the subject. (p.30)

The 2011 Ofsted report *History for All* also wholeheartedly supports this. It states:

In most of the history departments visited, teachers were using sub-levels in their assessments, usually in response to demands from senior leaders. This trend affected not only history but has also been noted in other foundation subjects, notably religious education and geography. Such practice was largely unhelpful since the levels were not intended for such minute differentiation or to be used so frequently. They were intended to be used sparingly and holistically to judge several pieces of work at the end of a key stage or, at most, at the end of a year. They were never intended to be used, as inspectors observed in some of the schools visited, to mark individual pieces of work. (pp.29–30)

This is really clear: level descriptors should not be used, and were not designed to be used, to assess individual pieces of work every six weeks. Teachers should not rely on this one type of assessment more than any other. But in reality this is what seems to be happening. One of the authors recently worked with a group of 30 teachers and asked them to put their hands up if they set their students half-termly assessments. They were then asked if they used the level descriptors to give the students a level or a sub-level which was recorded on a whole-school system. Depressingly, every single teacher put a hand up. When asked why, the main response was simply that it was whole-school policy. But as Lambert (2010: 1) points out, this is simply ridiculous:

> we have the commonplace absurdity of school teachers being instructed by senior leadership teams to create intermediate levels (e.g. level 3a, 3b, 3c etc). Fabricating such a quasi-scientific basis for reporting 'progress' to the SLT, parents and Ofsted has become in this way, let's face it, an enormous professional hoax.

Teachers are skilled professionals and we *do* assess all of the time through question-and-answer sessions, the marking of books, observing group work, the quality of homework. All of this data does inform our knowledge of the individual students that we teach. But how much does all of this valuable data inform our judgement of the levels that we give and which are fed into the whole-school database? Thompson (2009) argues this very point. He says that assessment should be viewed:

> as a series of different pieces of a jigsaw. Some sources of evidence offer greater clarity and accuracy but are only small pieces, limited in scope, giving a narrow view of pupils' overall understanding. Others offer more of the *big picture* of student attainment, but are more subjective and often heavily supported by the teacher.

Clearly when it comes to assessment in humanities subjects, practice has improved over recent years but some work still needs to be done. We should draw on the clear consensus about what constitutes good assessment when designing chunks of cross-curricular humanities work. We need to consider assessment that uses a variety of different sources of evidence and that has varying levels of reliability, and use this to inform our understanding of individual student need. The main aim of assessment is to help students improve. We also should use this varied information to inform our judgements when we record student attainment.

One of the key arguments within this book has been that, as you begin to consider adopting elements of a cross-curricular approach to teaching and learning, it is vital that you interrogate your own subject and its associated pedagogy with greater rigour. But what happens when schools try to take a different approach and do not interrogate their own subjects? As noted in Chapter 1 a number of schools have taken a competency-based approach to curriculum planning at KS3. This project-based approach often encompasses the humanities subjects, and some others besides. But how effective is assessment in helping students move forward in their understanding of the humanities subjects if schools use the freedom of the 2008 National Curriculum to innovate and take a more skills-based approach to their KS3 curricula? According to the RSA (2011), over 200 schools now teach the Opening Minds programme, and many of these courses incorporate humanities subjects. The framework for this curriculum is described here:

The Opening Minds curriculum features five categories of competences: learning, citizenship, relating to people, managing situations and managing information. Focusing on competences means that Opening Minds teaching emphasises the ability to understand and to do, rather than just the transmission of knowledge.

These competences are broad areas of capability, developed in classrooms through a mixture of instruction and practical experience: children plan their work, organise their own time and explore their own ways of learning.

Subject boundaries are less defined than in traditional curriculum teaching, with schools often integrating the teaching of several subjects together into modules or topics, where competences can be developed through the exploration of common themes. Crucially, the input of teachers and the individual needs of schools are central to the planning of each Opening Minds project.

The competences or skills that the Opening Minds project is structured around are also described on the RSA website, as discussed below.

Five key competences

Each competence category contains a number of individual competences, which are expressed in terms of what a school student could achieve having progressed through the curriculum.

Competences for citizenship

- *Morals and ethics* – students develop an understanding of ethics and values, how personal behaviour should be informed by these and how to contribute to society.

- *Making a difference* – students understand how society, government and business work, and the importance of active citizenship.

- *Diversity* – students understand and value social, cultural and community diversity, in both national and global contexts.

- *Technological impact* – students understand the social implications of technology.

- *Self-reliance* – students develop an understanding of how to manage aspects of their own lives and the techniques they might use to do so, including managing their financial affairs.

Competences for learning

- *Learning styles* – students understand different ways of learning and how to develop and assess their effectiveness as learners.

- *Reasoning* – students learn to think originally and systematically, and how to apply this knowledge.

- *Creativity* – students explore and understand their own abilities and creative talents, and how best to make use of them.

- *Positive motivation* – students learn to enjoy and love learning for its own sake and as part of understanding themselves.

- *Key skills* – students achieve high standards in literacy, numeracy and spatial understanding.
- *ICT skills* – students achieve high standards of competence in handling information and communications technology and understand the underlying processes.

Competences for managing information

- *Research* – students develop a range of techniques for accessing, evaluating and differentiating information, and have learned how to analyse, synthesise and apply it.
- *Reflection* – students understand the importance of reflecting and applying critical judgement, and learn how to do so.

Competences for relating to people

- *Leadership* – students understand how to relate to other people in varying contexts in which they might find themselves, including those where they manage, or are managed by, others; and how to get things done.
- *Teamwork* – students understand how to operate in teams and their own capacities for filling different team roles.
- *Coaching* – students understand how to develop other people, whether as peer or teacher.
- *Communication* – students develop a range of techniques for communicating by different means, and understand how and when to use them.
- *Emotional intelligence* – students develop competence in managing personal and emotional relationships.
- *Stress management* – students understand and are able to use varying means of managing stress and conflict.

Competences for managing situations

- *Time management* – students understand the importance of managing their own time, and develop preferred techniques for doing so.
- *Coping with change* – students understand what is meant by managing change, and develop a range of techniques for use in varying situations.
- *Feelings and reactions* – students understand the importance both of celebrating success and managing disappointment, and ways of handling these.
- *Creative thinking* – students understand what is meant by being entrepreneurial and initiative-taking, and how to develop their capacities in these areas.
- *Risk taking* – students understand how to manage risk and uncertainty, including the wide range of contexts in which these will be encountered and techniques for managing them. (http://www.rsaopeningminds.org.uk/)

Practical task 7.1

A school is considering delivering humanities subjects at KS3 through a competency-based curriculum as advocated by the RSA (see above). They want to integrate history, geography, RE and citizenship and deliver these subjects through the five different competences, taking a thematic approach. They are mindful that they need to get assessment in classrooms right, and that they need to report progress to the students so that the students can see where they need to improve. What advice would you offer them?

As you read through the case study lesson below, think about how far this school seems to have considered assessment when it came to long-term, medium-term and short-term planning. What could be done to improve this school's approach to assessment?

Case study 7.1: *What should be assessed in a competency lesson on the weather?*

Orange School has adopted a competency-based curriculum for Year 7 and Year 8 based on the RSA's Opening Minds course. As in Pear College, described in Chapter 2, each half term is focused on a different project, including 'Our community', 'A sense of place' and 'World weather'. Through these projects pupils are expected to develop a range of competences (as above), improve levels of motivation, enhance their literacy skills and learn history, geography, RE, PSHE, citizenship and ICT. The belief is that if students are taught certain competences in the early years of secondary education their progress will accelerate when it comes to studying the humanities subjects in the more traditional manner at Key Stage 4. The head teacher and teachers of the competency-based course at Orange School are totally committed to this belief. We were able to visit the school, observe the curriculum in action, talk to the teachers and look closely at assessment.

The best lesson that was observed on the visit was taught to Year 8. The teacher wanted the students to understand how and why different areas across the world have extreme weather conditions. The students were to learn the answers to these two questions through case study work. Each group worked on its particular case study then presented its findings to the rest of the class. Groups were reminded by the teacher of key competences that they had used before and which they might use in their research; words such as 'thinking logically', 'investigating' and 'analysing' were mentioned. However, these words were not explained or exemplified. When we asked a number of students what they meant, they did not know.

The students were given resource packs for their particular case study and then provided with key questions to guide their research. After about ten minutes of research the teacher told the class that they had to present their findings as a written report that would be assessed. The teacher then quickly displayed the relevant English Assessing Pupil Progress Assessment Focus to try to model what progress might look like in report writing. Then, after less than a minute the teacher flashed up the geography level descriptors to show the class what level they were aiming for in geography. When the students were asked if this was helpful, they said they did not have the time to read and therefore make sense of either the English or the geography level descriptions.

As we know the levels were never intended to be used to assess individual tasks, nor is the language in them accessible to many students. All of this information put together confused the class. Were they writing an English report? Were they trying to show their understanding of geography? Were they being assessed on how well they were researching as a group? If they were writing a report as a group, which person was going to write it? Were they all going to be judged on this one person's efforts?

When the students were asked if they understood the task, they were unclear about what they had to do in general. They were also unclear about what information they needed to extrapolate from the resource packs to use to write their reports. When asked what information they were looking for one student said, 'I don't really know.' Another was simply copying information, much of which was irrelevant. In discussion with the teacher after the lesson, he too was unclear. He said that assessment in the competences has always been an issue. They had not yet formed an agreed system to record progress in the competences. Nor was he a trained geography, history or RE teacher, so he had limited understanding of what to assess from a subject-specific perspective.

Of course it is quite possible to help students improve their literacy levels and write a well-structured report which demonstrates good geographical understanding. It is also desirable for students to work well together as a group. All of these are sound objectives. But without really modelling how to do this, or clearly understanding what good geographical understanding looks like, or being clear whether all or some of the group members should produce the written report, the assessment practices used in this lesson were confusing for the students.

It became clear from other lesson observations that the teachers were able to use certain types of formative assessment such as monitoring group work, sharing objectives and using question-and-answer sessions to check learning. However, other elements of formative assessment, notably modelling, appeared to be missing from their teachers' toolkit. It was clear that modelling would have been hugely beneficial to the students, enabling them to see explicitly how to go about the task. The team would have benefited from talking to their English colleagues to help develop such pedagogical approaches.

Crucially, when it came to assessing student progress there was confusion. The teachers were not teaching history or geography or RE in the traditional sense, although these subjects were subsumed in the course. When asked individually to identify the concepts and processes that underpin any one of the humanities subjects, as described in the 2008 National Curriculum, not a single member of staff knew any. They did not seem to understand that the humanities subjects should be taught as disciplines. They did not or could not draw on the teaching expertise of humanities teachers that existed within the school, nor could they discuss assessment practice with them because they were teaching something different. The teachers seemed to see history, geography or RE as just content to be used to teach the RSA's competences. The team were not assessing or recording the students' progress in their conceptual understanding of any of the humanities subjects. Nor were they sure of what to assess in the competences they were teaching. Clearly the team needed, when they first decided to adopt the competency-based curriculum, to think more about progression and assessment in the five competences they were teaching.

In Chapter 1 we argued that it is vital that any cross-curricular approaches to teaching humanities subjects should be based upon a clear understanding of the subject areas, and the thinking and discipline that underpins them. When it comes to assessment, this kind of understanding is critical. In the case study above, the school had not thought through exactly what to assess in their new curriculum, or how to do so. This was still causing issues over a year into the course. How would your advice from task 1 help them? As we stated in Chapter 2, working out what progression means in generic skills is a very challenging task. But it can be done. However, time and thought need to be invested here. This type of thinking is crucial, and needs be addressed early in the curriculum planning process.

Good assessment must be seen as part of the whole process of teaching and learning. It should flow from the main learning activities pupils have been engaged in and it should be planned for, preferably across the curriculum. It is difficult to do this without having a clear understanding of the thinking and discipline that underpins each humanities subject. If schools adopt a competency approach and integrate humanities subjects within this, they need to be clear about what it is they are teaching when it comes to substantive and procedural knowledge. This will help inform them how and what to assess, and how this data should be recorded and reported back to the students. After all it is very difficult to design teaching and learning activities – and therefore assessment activities – without knowing exactly what knowledge and concepts/processes we are teaching.

We would argue that this level of understanding is vital to teach our own subjects better, and that it is also vital if we want to take a more integrated approach to the curriculum. We would also argue that assessment must go hand in hand with a clear view of what progression looks like in our subject disciplines and in the competences that we choose to deliver. When we have this kind of understanding we can plan across a longer period of time, say from three to five years, and really consider how, when and in what context our teaching will help our students make progress, and when we should reinforce earlier learning.

Practical task 7.2

As a subject specialist you have a firm grasp of exactly what it is that you want to assess in your subject. But do you know what other humanities teachers are aiming to assess in their subjects? Individually, write down what you think should be assessed in a different humanities subject from your own. Then compare your thoughts with a subject expert. This will help you focus more on what it is you should be assessing, as well as helping you understand what other colleagues are aiming to assess.

What is progression?

Counsell (1999: 2) claimed that, 'if we have no personal sense of what getting better in history means then we may as well give up and go home.' She really hits the nail on the head here. If we want to help our students achieve and become better at the humanities subjects, we should be spending much of our time thinking about what progression looks like. But how often do departments actually sit down and think about what progression is and what it looks like in the classroom? When was the last time you did this? Is progression merely remembering more factual knowledge? Extending one's vocabulary? Better literacy skills? If progression is related to understanding (and we think it has to be), what characterises better understanding of key concepts such as 'causation' or 'place'? Is it about students moving from being dependent on the teacher to becoming more independent?

Let us start with some definitions. According to Weedon and Butt (2010: 10–11): 'Progression is the measurable advances in knowledge, understanding and skills made by pupils in their studies over time.' Vermeulen (2000: 38) observed that: 'Progress can perhaps be summed up as an increasing sophisticated understanding of history.' Lee and Shemilt (2003: 22) stated that progression should be viewed as 'the gradual transformation of misconceptions rather than as the gradual accumulation of correction ideas'. Put in simple terms, progression means getting better at history or geography or RE. This sounds fine in theory. But if we don't think hard enough about how children make progress then we may end up with a curriculum described by Butt (Weedon and Butt, 2009: 10–11) that has:

> Elements of continuity (featuring similar geographical content, concepts, themes, skills, etc year on year), but poor progression – typically covering the same ground, without expecting pupils to make intellectual advances as they mature. Here pupils would progress essentially by learning the same things, but maybe in a slightly different context.

In this sense teachers 'do' Italy in Year 7 then 'do' Japan in Year 8, then 'do' Kenya in Year 9 without thinking about how to develop a more sophisticated level of understanding. The curriculum in this case can be just viewed as content to be delivered. Unfortunately it appears that this may be a reality for a number of geography departments. As the 2011 Ofsted report, *Geography: Learning to make a world of difference*, stated:

> Teachers made much better use of assessment to establish what students knew and could do and to identify what progress they needed to make. What was less well developed, however, and what schools needed to focus on was how best to ensure that the students actually made progress. (p.29)

So how should we tackle this thorny issue of helping students to make progress? Clearly the National Curriculum level descriptors are no good here. As discussed above, they were only ever meant to be used as summative statements at the end of KS3 to make a best-fit judgement. When studied closely, they do not give us enough detail about what getting better at the different elements of humanities subjects looks like. There are alternative and arguably better ways for us to think about progression. But where do we start? We should be helping students make progress in general terms. Clear advice has been given. Lomas (1990) has demonstrated that it is possible to identify certain signposts for progression in history which you can apply to the setting and marking of your pupils work:

- greater historical knowledge with which to substantiate statements and judgements;
- ability to categorise, see patterns, summarise and generalise; a grasp of essentials from a mass of detail;
- ability to make connections and links between issues and problems of different periods, including the present; the ability to focus on the most significant issues; an increasing awareness of the relevance of the topic and its wider significance;
- the ability to move from concrete to abstract concepts;
- the ability to explain rather than just describe;
- the ability to be precise, a concern for accuracy and the limitations of accuracy indicative of clarity of thought;
- an independence of thought, ability to pose questions, hypothesise, devise ways of finding answers;
- to have an informed scepticism, an inclination to qualify statements with elements of uncertainty, yet still be prepared to reach conclusions.

Maybe progression should be thought about more from the point of view of a teacher's input as Telfer (2004) demonstrates (see Table 7.1). He argues that progression comes from how much teachers do compared with how much the students do. Eventually we should aim for our students to, at certain points in the curriculum, be designing and conducting their own enquiries.

Table 7.1 'Geographical Enquiry & Progression in Teaching Styles', by kind permission of Steve Telfer

Stage of teaching and learning	Closed	Framed	Negotiated
Questions	Questions not explicit, or questions remain the teacher's questions.	Questions explicit, activities planned to make children ask questions.	Children decide what they want to investigate under guidance from teacher.
Data	Data selected by teacher, presented as authoritative, not to be challenged.	Variety of data selected by teacher, presented as evidence to be interpreted.	Children are helped to find their own data from sources in and out of school.
Interpretation	Teacher decides what is to be done with data, children follow instructions.	Methods of interpretation are open to discussion and choice.	Children chose methods of analysis and interpretation in consultation with teacher.
Conclusion	Key ideas presented, generalisations are predicted, not open to debate.	Children reach conclusions from data, different interpretations are expected.	Children reach their own conclusions and evaluate them.
Summary	Teacher controls the knowledge by making all decisions about data, activities and conclusions. Children are not expected to challenge what is presented.	The teacher inducts children into ways in which geographical knowledge is constructed, so that they are able to use these ways to construct knowledge themselves. Children are made aware of choices and are encouraged to become critical.	Children are enabled by the teacher to investigate questions of concern and interest to themselves.

Source: Adapted from Roberts (2003).

How can we plan for progression?

We also need to think about progression from a procedural point of view. But how should we do this? Can we separate out the main organising concepts that make up our subjects and think about what progression looks like in each one? Should this look like some kind of ladder? Or as suggested by Byrom (2003), are they more like a climbing frame than a learning ladder?

Practical task 7.3

To do this task you need first to work on your own, then with a teacher from your own subject and finally, if available, with a teacher of another humanities subject. If we are to understand what progression is we should understand what concepts we want our children to develop as well as what knowledge we want to impart.

1. Without looking at the National Curriculum, list all of the main concepts and processes that make up your subject discipline.

2. Check your list with a colleague who is a specialist in the same subject area. Are your concepts the same? Did you have any differences? Check to see if you have the same concepts as the National Curriculum – see page 14 of Chapter 1 if you are not sure.

3. Where do you teach these different concepts and processes in your curriculum? Take one concept; what do you expect Year 7 to able to do? How will you have developed this understanding for Year 9 and further developed it for Year 11?

4. How and where do you assess students' understanding of these particular concepts?

5. Now ask a colleague from a different humanities subject if they know what the main concepts and processes are that underpin your specialist subject? Where they have gaps in their knowledge, you need to explain to them what the concepts are and give an example of the context in which you teach them.

This activity will help you work out how much you know about your own subject discipline and how much you know about the true nature of the other humanities subjects. You may well be surprised how much you know. Case Studies 2 and 3 below could reassure you here. It may well be worth revisiting question 5 when you have finished reading them.

Case study 7.2: *Planning for progression and assessment in history at KS3*

Here one of the authors describes his experience of creating a working party in 2009/2010 to develop ideas for planning for progression in history and linking this to assessment.

The group was made up of four history teachers: two subject leaders – one from a boys' school performing at roughly the national average based on whole-school GCSE data, another from a high-achieving comprehensive in an affluent area – one Assistant Head Teacher from a national challenge school and one classroom teacher from a school with more than the average number of children on free school meals. We met on four different occasions throughout the year. Our mission was simple: to improve our practice by planning for progression in history. We wanted to explore what progression might look like in the long term and consider how a deeper understanding of progression might affect our curriculum planning. We also wanted to think about how this understanding might affect the way we assess work on a day-to-day basis and over a longer period of time so that we could give meaningful feedback to students to help them improve. We also wanted to standardise the judgements we made in order to create a rational approach to assessment which could be shared across the county. This project was based on a similar project completed in Hampshire when I was a head of history under the watchful eye of the then County History Inspector, Neil Thompson, in 2002.

At the first meeting the group agreed progression was more than just learning and remembering more historical information. They felt that it was equally about helping the students to get better at the different key elements of history. At this point I asked the group what were the main key elements or concepts and processes that make up history. Individually they had to write a list. Only then were they able to check with each other to see if they were in agreement. Interestingly they all were. As individuals they came up with all but one of the concepts (namely cultural, religious and ethnic diversity). This consensus in understanding what makes up history as a school subject was clear. History teachers do seem to have this agreed view. As a teaching community they seem to understand what makes up the discipline of the subject. Since the introduction of the National Curriculum, its statutory orders for history have not seen huge changes to what are regarded as the organising concepts. Certain concepts have developed over time, such as the understanding of what constitutes historical interpretations and the place of historical significance. But in general terms, the second-order concepts for history have stayed the same.

The next task for the group was to think about the entire key stage. Where did they teach the different concepts and processes? The teachers realised that when teaching an enquiry or a lesson, often they would be dealing with more than one of the concepts. However, all agreed that some lessons had a concept that was its major focus, while others were more peripheral. The group was asked to plot on a grid where and in what context they taught the different concepts between Years 7 and 9. They were also asked to think whether or not they were encouraging the students' thinking within each concept to become more sophisticated over time, or was the work just pitched at the same level in a variety of contexts? The results of this mini-audit were revealing. All of the teachers' curricula were very causation heavy. They all noticed that interpretations and significance were very thin on the ground in comparison. In two cases the teachers did not really teach significance at all, and one teacher only really taught interpretations in any meaningful way once. Discussions revealed that they were secure in their own understanding of what made good causation work, but were less secure in their understanding of what constituted high-level thinking in interpretations and significance. Two interesting by-products also emerged from this mini-audit. Firstly, the teachers noticed that the end task they nearly always set to assess students' understanding for causation was an extended piece of writing, more commonly known as an essay. We discussed the effects that this might have on the students' motivation, especially for those who struggled with literacy, and on their own marking load. We then considered different ways in which the students could show their understanding. Secondly, the teacher in the boys' school noticed that his curriculum was focused very much on military and political history, whereas the female teacher from a mixed school noticed that her curriculum was centred much more around social issues. Were the teachers choosing content to best fit their learners, or were they choosing the content that they were most interested in?

The next challenge was to focus on interpretations, one of the more difficult concepts. After defining what interpretations are, and discussing what they were not, the group was encouraged to think about what they wanted their brightest students to understand about interpretations when they finished studying history. The group agreed that in some ways separating the concepts out to think about progression was not necessarily the right thing to do. However, we agreed that it would become too messy and too complicated to try and think about progression in all of the second-order concepts at the same time. The teachers scribbled their ideas on different post-it notes. When we had exhausted our thoughts we tried to arrange the post-its into some kind of hierarchy: which ideas were easy and which were more difficult to get across to the students. After a few minutes we realised that this was potentially the wrong way to go about things. We couldn't really decide which ideas were easier or harder to get across without knowing the context in which the idea was being taught. After all it is arguably much harder to analyse the stylistic devices used in a 400-page history book than it is in a 40-word commemorative wall plaque. However, we did notionally create a hierarchy of ideas – see Figure 7.1. It was much more important to ensure that each interpretation's idea that we wanted to get across to our students, was covered in a variety of contexts across the key stage. We also realised that in our long-term planning we needed to take into account the difficulty of the idea and the chosen context, and ensure that this was taught when individual departments felt their the students were ready.

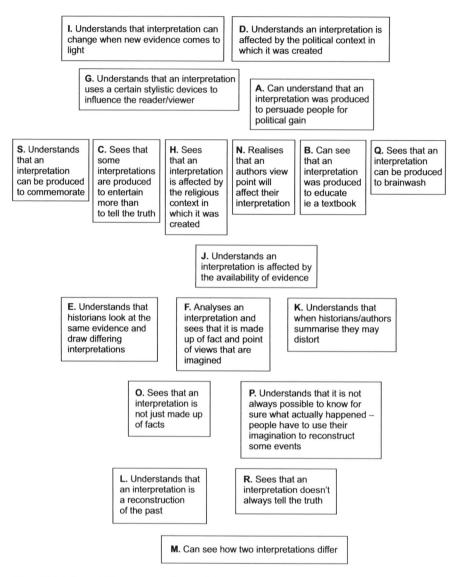

Figure 7.1 Interpretations progression model

By this point of the project it was time to get down to the practical work of creating some history lessons that 'hit' certain elements of interpretations from our progression model. The lessons needed to teach and allow students to learn some selected aspects of interpretations from Figure 7.1. The lessons also needed to finish with a meaningful end product which could be more formally assessed. This didn't have to be an essay or an extended piece of writing. Also, the teachers were asked to create a precise mark scheme which would allow them to clearly assess the end product. The mark scheme needed to show other teachers assessing the end products what low, medium, high and highest levels of understanding might look like in this context (see Burnham and Brown, 2004). Also, the teachers were encouraged to give examples of student responses in the mark schemes to help other teachers decide how they might decide on attainment in different pieces of work. We agreed that in all probability, when they had assessed the work, the mark schemes would change and be adapted the light of student responses.

The group also had to decide how much teacher input there should be in these particular end tasks. After all, if the students are told exactly what to write and what to include, and the work is modelled for them, who has shown their understanding, the teacher or the student? Here there was much disagreement. One teacher felt that the students did need support and guidance to complete the tasks. Others mainly agreed with Thompson (2009) that the most reliable data would be gleaned if these tasks were short and 'unseen'. We came to the conclusion as a group that both approaches were fine. Good teachers do need to model and show how students should approach certain tasks. But, at certain points across the key stage, we agreed that it is vital to be able to see exactly what students can do independently. Taking all of this assessment data as a whole helps inform our understanding of student progress.

We also agreed that we needed to ensure that across the key stage, teachers delivered and revisited all aspects of the interpretations in Figure 7.1 through different enquiries. A model of what this might look like, taken from McFahn (2011) is shown below in Figure 7.2.

Who was the Real Richard the Lionheart? Interpretation type: modern film	Why bother with the Black Death? Interpretation type: quotes from two historians	How should we commemorate Peterloo? Interpretation type: commemorative plaque	What really happened in November 1971? Interpretation type: histories prose and a silent film
What parts of the interpretation are factual/points of view/imagined? What is the relationship between the interpretation and the available evidence? What was the purpose/intended audience of the interpretation?	What is the relationship between the interpretation and the available evidence?	What does an interpretation say or show (style and tone)? What parts of the interpretation are factual/points of view/imagined? What is the relationship between the interpretation and the available evidence? How was the interpretation affected by the context in which it was created? What was the intended audience of the interpretation?	What does an interpretation say or show (style and tone)? What parts of the interpretation are factual/points of view/imagined? What is the relationship between the interpretation and the available evidence? How was the interpretation affected by the context in which it was created? What was the intended audience of the interpretation?

Figure 7.2 Progression in interpretations

At the end of the project three of the teachers felt that the work had helped them shift their thinking about teaching history. It had made them understand the importance of understanding progression as it informs curriculum planning, teaching and assessment.

Case study 7.3: *Planning for progression and assessment in geography at KS3*

Here one of the authors reflects on a similar process to the case study described above, this time working with geography teachers.

Running alongside the history working party described in case study 2 was a similar group made up of seven geography teachers. Four of these were chosen because they were Advanced Skills Teachers, and three were, judging by GCSE results, highly successful curriculum leaders. We also met on four different occasions throughout the year. Our mission was the same as the history group's, as described above: to improve our practice by planning for progression in geography, to explore what progression might look like in the long term and consider how a deeper understanding of progression might affect our curriculum planning. We also wanted to think about how this understanding might affect the way we assess work on a day-to-day basis and over a longer period of time so that we could give meaningful feedback to students to help them improve. We also wanted to standardise the judgements we made in order to create a rational approach to assessment which could be shared across the county.

As the group facilitator I took exactly the same approach to the sessions as I did with the history group. However, the discussions and outcomes which followed were hugely different. At the first meeting the group was asked if they could individually list the main concepts and processes, as described in the 2008 National Curriculum, that make up geography as a subject. The teachers sat in silence for two or three minutes. Then they all agreed that they couldn't come up with them individually. Could they manage to identify the concepts as a group? They did come up with a number of the concepts but not all. They found this exercise hugely difficult and quite demoralising. Why was this? Perhaps it stems from the fact that the 2008 National Curriculum orders look to geography teachers so different from those from 1999. Although the concepts are similar, they were not as prominent in 1999 and the curriculum appeared to be more prescriptive and detailed. Therefore there is not a consensus view of what geography is amongst the geography teaching community. Or did it prove Lambert and Morgan's point (2010: 45)?

> One of the backwash effects of the National Curriculum in 1988 was to lay down 'statutory orders' for each subject including geography. This gave the impression that subject knowledge was under the direct control

of the government and/or agencies. In effect what happened was that teachers surrendered a crucial aspect of their identities – ceding to the state decisions about what to teach. Teacher energy had been redirected to assimilating ever more complex requirements and guidance on pedagogy and assessment. There is relatively little incentive to engage in the subject.

When asked to review their present KS3 curricula and plot where they taught the different concepts and processes, the geography teachers also struggled to do this. The history teachers realised that some lessons or enquiries had more than one conceptual focus, but could see where the different organising concepts featured. The geography teachers felt that they could not do this at all. One teacher mentioned that they didn't think about their subject in this way; rather they taught geography through case studies of places and in those particular case studies 'did' or taught all of the geography.

When we attempted to think about what progression might look like in the different concepts as laid down in the National Curriculum of 2008, again we struggled as a group. The majority of the group felt that the task had already been done because they used the National Curriculum level descriptors and these were adequate. When it was pointed out to them that the levels were never designed to be used in this way, some felt that if SLTs were happy to use them then we should continue to do so. Further meaningful professional discussions took place. One teacher, determined to think about the problem and come to some kind of agreed understanding beyond the level descriptors, stated that if we could not think about progression through the main concepts of geography then maybe geography is not a subject discipline at all?

An alternate view that emerged was that progression needs to be seen in terms of complexity and content rather than of concept. The argument was that when looking at decision-making activities the same skills were used but progression came when one thought about size and scale. An activity for Year 7 may ask students where to place a pedestrian crossing on a particular street. The students need to consider a range of factors that affect this in a localised area. The same task can be made increasingly difficult by changing the scale and the size. If the task asks where an airport should be sited, the students are using the same skills but the size and scale of the task make it more complicated. They need to consider more factors and more points of view. Despite introducing the work of Taylor (2008), who modelled how to plan enquiries around the main organising concepts of geography, the group could not agree on what progression would look like within the main organising concepts. As a specialist history teacher I did not have the necessary experience to help decide if this is approach was asking the impossible or not.

Like the history group, the geographers were then asked to create some meaningful lessons which 'hit' or taught the different concepts. The lessons also needed to result in a meaningful end product which could be assessed. Again this did not have to be an essay or an extended piece of writing. Also, the teachers were asked to create a precise mark scheme. This scheme needed to show other teachers who were assessing the end products what low, medium, high and highest levels of understanding might look like in this context.

At the end of the project some of the teachers' understanding of progression and assessment had shifted. One teacher really felt that designing tasks with an end product which she could assess using a bespoke mark scheme had really improved her understanding of how to plan, teach and assess. Another teacher agreed. He realised that marking and giving National Curriculum levels for individual pieces of work was a nonsense and he went on to totally change his department's assessment policy, so that feedback for benchmark assessments would be given in terms of written comments, based on well-thought-through activities and individually designed mark schemes. But some of the teachers really struggled to think about progression in terms of concepts. They also found it difficult to see the need for creating progression models when we had the National Curriculum level descriptors to call upon.

Practical task 7.4

In Chapter 2 we suggested one focus for a cross-curricular chunk of work could be on contested places, such as the Middle East. Geography could help the students understand what this place is like today. History could provide the historical context for an understanding of the issues surrounding those who live in the region, whilst the topic opens up possibilities for RE to study different religions and issues of interfaith dialogue and ethics, and citizenship could look at the range of actions that could be taken to resolve tension in the region. Imagine that this work is to be taught to Year 8. Working as a subject specialist, identify the concepts and processes that you would want to focus on in such a cross-curricular piece of work. How is this harder than previous work? If you can compare this with teachers from the other humane subjects, you can create a plan for a meaningful chunk of cross-curricular work.

Conclusions

Working with the teachers in the two case studies highlighted just how challenging it is for subject specialists to think about what progression looks in their own subject disciplines. This is partly because it is indeed difficult. What makes it more challenging is the fact that many colleagues have not had the time or opportunity to think in this way before. Moreover, like many other teachers, humanities specialists have unwittingly bought into what Lambert and Morgan (2010) describe above as the 'enormous professional hoax' that is using the level descriptors as meaningful measures of and models for progression. But really thinking hard about how our students make progress in general and specific terms in our subject disciplines, and then planning this out across three or five years, is vital if we actually want to help them make real progress. We should also consider what this looks like in classroom activities, and how we check to see whether our students have made the progress we have planned for. It is only when we have had time to do this type of thinking that we can really explore with other specialists the common areas where we might take cross-curricular approaches to learning. If not, the work students produce in class may well be superficial and they may not really be learning rigorous history or geography or RE.

Can we realistically expect non-specialist teachers, who are sometimes asked to teach an integrated humanities course or a competency-based course, to do this kind of thinking? Can they be expected to plan for progression to happen in different subject disciplines and then assess to see whether this progress has been made? Should they be doing this as well as thinking about what progression might look like in the different competences they are expected to teach and plan for in their courses? Clearly all of this would be very difficult, and a potentially daunting task for individual teachers to face. If this is the case, *how do we* ensure that the humanities subjects are being delivered well, that progress is being properly measured and that students understand how to develop their skills in an integrated curriculum?

Is it better to take a more interdisciplinary approach to curriculum planning, where specialist teachers teach within their specialisms whilst working under a theme or a topic that cuts across the subjects? If this is the case, then we need to encourage subject specialists to think about what progression in their particular subject means to them. This is challenging yet vital work. Teachers need to be given the time and support to do this kind of thinking and planning. If we do not engage with the thorny issue of progression, and how we assess and measure this, then perhaps Counsell is correct: 'we should give up and go home.' And none of us want to do that because the humanities subjects are too important!

Professional standards for QTS

QTS Standards: Q6, Q11, Q12, Q14, Q15, Q22, Q25, Q26, Q27, Q28, Q29, Q32.

Professional standards for teachers

Core Standards: C6, C11, C12, C14, C15, C26, C29, C30, C31, C32, C33, C34, C35, C36.

8

Future directions

Key objectives

By the end of this chapter, you will have:

- reviewed the differing ways in which humanities subjects can engage with the principles and practices of cross-curricular teaching and learning;
- engaged with the current and changing external influences on the curriculum and understood how these are likely to impact upon longer-term decisions about cross-curricular teaching and learning;
- identified aspects of a teaching pedagogy for the humanities that would remain relevant and empowering in future educational climates;
- discussed the conclusion that it is viable to maintain the integrity of subjects within a framework that gives each of the humanities a different way of looking at the world and a different form of knowledge, each of which is valuable, but which are mutually beneficial.

A metaphor for a cross-curricular disposition

In the core book of this series, *Cross-Curricular Teaching and Learning in the Secondary School*, Jonathan Savage concludes with an exploration of a range of metaphors and applies these to possible future opportunities for developing cross-curricular work (Savage, 2011). In this chapter we aim to recap these, test their application to the areas we have explored in this humanities-specific title, and then return to them at the end to draw conclusions about the possible future direction for cross-curricular working in the humanities.

Savage uses Isaiah Berlin's famous essay 'The hedgehog and the fox' as an initial metaphor to explore the tension between different dispositions towards the secondary curriculum. Berlin takes the attributed phrase of Ancient Greek poet Archilochus that 'The fox knows many little things, but the hedgehog knows one big thing' and develops this in the following passage:

Scholars have differed about the correct interpretation of these dark words, which may mean no more than that the fox, for all his cunning, is defeated by the hedgehog's one defence. But, taken figuratively, the words can be made to yield a sense in which they mark one of the deepest differences which divide writers and thinkers, and, it may be, human beings in general.

For there exists a great chasm between those, on one side, who relate everything to a single central vision, one system, less or more coherent or articulate, in terms of which they understand, think and feel – a single, universal, organising principle in terms of which alone all that they are and say has significance – and, on the other side, those who pursue many ends, often unrelated and even contradictory, connected, if at all, only in some de facto way, for some psychological or physiological cause, related to no moral or aesthetic principle. These last lead lives, perform acts and entertain ideas that are centrifugal rather than centripetal; their thought is scattered or diffused, moving on many levels, seizing upon the essence of a vast variety of experiences and objects for what they are in themselves, without, consciously or unconsciously, seeking to fit them into, or exclude them from, any one unchanging, all-embracing, sometimes self-contradictory and incomplete, at times fanatical, unitary inner vision. The first kind of intellectual and artistic personality belongs to the hedgehogs, the second to the foxes.

(Berlin, 1953: 1–2)

Berlin's contention is therefore that human beings can be categorised as either 'hedgehogs' or 'foxes', in that hedgehogs' lives are dominated by a single, central vision of reality through which they think and feel. Foxes, in contrast, live what might be called a centrifugal life, pursuing many divergent ends. Berlin goes on to give examples of each type. Whilst exploring the benefits and problems of being on either side of this intellectual divide, Savage (2011: 168–70) concludes that 'teaching seems dominated by hedgehogs. We need more foxes' (pp.168–9).

Reflective task 8.1

Savage offers a chance to develop your understanding of this idea with a chance to personally position yourself in this 'divide'. As a bit of light relief, do you think you are a hedgehog or a fox? A short quiz will help you find out: http://jsavage.org.uk/?p=528. Decide whether you agree or disagree with the 12 statements presented and follow the instructions to work out your score. Do not take it too seriously!

It is easy to see how this metaphor can be applied to curriculum development in recent times, as has been explored in Chapter 1 when looking at the prevalence of overarching curriculum models that seek to sweep away subject 'boundaries' in favour of broader competencies.

Savage goes on to structure questions about the future of cross-curricular teaching and learning within a wider consideration of the possible future of this over the next 15 years, using three main headings:

- a renaissance of curriculum development;
- the pull towards centrifugal teaching;
- the future possibilities for cross-curricular teaching and learning.

The first of these is particularly interesting as it resolves into a metaphor based on Renaissance polyphonic music:

> Renaissance polyphonic music expressed the metaphors or universal orderliness and interdependence within a perfect musical form. The result of this approach was the most beautiful religious music, characterised by its many interweaving parts sounding as one that can be heard, daily, in cathedrals and other large churches. For our Renaissance curriculum model, this type of subject polyphony would be something to aspire to. It would permeate through our Renaissance curriculum model by allowing key knowledge, skills and understanding which are initiated by individual subjects (voices) to be shared across subjects (between voices) in a way that allows them to exist alongside each other with an equal sense of value. It could allow particular subjects to take the lead at particular times, but always within a combined, overall sense of balance, purpose and direction. It could highlight a specific theme for a certain period, sharing it amongst subjects and allowing each to present it with its own particular subject tone or resonance. It could handle potential clashes of knowledge or learning by carefully preparing learners for the potential dissonance, allowing them to enjoy the creative tension that the dissonance allows before resolving it for them in a sensitively managed and appropriate way.
>
> (Savage, 2011: 177)

This could be seen as a curriculum model, but in reality is more a set of dispositions a teacher might need to possess in order to create such a vision. However it might be interpreted, it leads Savage to briefly consider a style of teaching that might facilitate this: 'centrifugal teaching' in which teachers are outward looking and therefore less concerned about a final framework or meaning. Here we return to our 'foxes' and the centrifugal disposition, in that such teaching within a 'renaissance curriculum' model will lead to the development of a successful cross-curricular pedagogy.

Finally, this leads Savage to reflect on the future possibilities for cross-curricular teaching and learning. He sees the medium to long-term challenges in the possibility that individual subjects may simply cease to exist and therefore, in order to ensure subjects remain relevant, teachers will need to 're-think the ways in which subject knowledge contributes to these new curriculum and pedagogical frameworks' (Savage, 2011: 180).

The changing educational landscape

So where does this leave us in the humanities? To begin with Savage's final point on the potential demise of the subject, it is worth putting this into the context of current curriculum changes. Naturally, it is hard to write anything on this without it immediately becoming a hostage to fortune. Governments and associated 'quangos' have constantly revised and adjusted the National Curriculum since its inception, and at the time of writing the situation is no different. A full-scale review of the National Curriculum, announced in January 2011, will eventually lead to new programmes of study for history and geography in 2014, and at the time of writing the outcomes are still unclear. Doubtless there will be an impact on RE agreed syllabi, and citizenship seems very unlikely to continue at all as a discrete subject in the curriculum.

It is, however, possible to identify some important changes that are going to take place and consider how these might impact, positively or negatively, on cross-curricular learning in the humanities.

One change already occurring is the 'English Baccalaureate'. Introduced initially as a performance tables measure from January 2011, its stated aim is to encourage more pupils to study 'academic' subjects. To achieve the 'Baccalaureate' pupils must achieve a GCSE grade C or above in English, maths, science, a modern or ancient language and a humanities subject. However for the purposes of this, a humanities subject is defined as only history or geography. Inevitably the status of geography and history will be raised, even more so if this becomes certificated as is intended. Given the specific end-of-KS4 goal of a C or above, this is likely to discourage cross-curricular approaches as a league-table-driven focus on preparation for the end product stretches down into KS3. This also raises the question: what about RE, or for that matter citizenship? There can be little incentive for schools to develop the curriculum in these areas when the rewards are clearly tied to geography and history, and this is likely to have an impact on cross-curricular working.

As regards the new National Curriculum, the Secretary of State for education Michael Gove gave a clear indication in his speech to the Conservative party conference in October 2010 of the direction changes will take when attacking history teaching:

> But then, how many of our students are learning the lessons of history?
> One of the under-appreciated tragedies of our time has been the sundering of our society from its past.
>
> Children are growing up ignorant of one of the most inspiring stories I know – the history of our United Kingdom.
>
> Our history has moments of pride, and shame, but unless we fully understand the struggles of the past we will not properly value the liberties of the present.
>
> The current approach we have to history denies children the opportunity to hear our island story. Children are given a mix of topics at primary, a cursory run through Henry the Eighth and Hitler at secondary and many give up the subject at 14, without knowing how the vivid episodes of our past become a connected narrative. Well, this trashing of our past has to stop.
>
> (Gove, 2010)

This, and subsequent statements, indicate a clear move towards a narrative approach, in which a core body of knowledge is defined and passed on to pupils. Similar references have been made to rivers and capital cities in geography. Naturally the situation is different with RE, given that locally agreed arrangements are to remain. Citizenship has not featured in government statements, a further indication of its likely demise, although schools will still have the freedom to cover it if they wish.

Whilst it will be 2013 before any of the new programmes of study for the humanities subjects are available, we already know that they will be slimmed down and focus on core knowledge, with the 2010 White Paper 'The importance of teaching' stating:

> We want the National Curriculum to be a benchmark not a straitjacket, a body of knowledge against which achievement can be measured. The new National Curriculum will therefore have a greater focus on subject content, outlining the essential knowledge and understanding that pupils should be expected to have to enable them to take their place as educated members of society. Teachers must be free to use their professionalism and expertise to support all children to progress. So, in outlining what children should expect to know in core subjects, the new curriculum will allow a greater degree of freedom in how that knowledge might be acquired and what other teaching should complement this core.
>
> (DfE, 2010)

What will this mean for future curriculum planning? A clearly defined range of core knowledge in each subject may trouble teachers on both a philosophical and practical level. However this could make an easier starting point for joint planning. Each subject specialist will be able to easily access the core content the others are studying, and such cooperation could be especially effective if careful thought is given to where subjects could usefully combine in the drafting of this in the different subject areas. Coupled with a renewed emphasis on 'subjects', this ought to spell the end for the some of the looser content-free models that have passed for cross-curricular work in some schools. The Personal, Learning and Thinking Skills (PLTS) are also absent from these plans, which may emphasise the need to give curriculum innovation a distinctly subject-specific flavour. Combine this with the greater freedoms offered by this new curriculum and there seems little to suggest than the 2014 National Curriculum will in any way hinder the development of cross-curricular teaching and learning in the humanities.

Of course, should specified content prove to be excessive this could present problems. If the humanities subjects once again feel under pressure to 'get through' the content, this may come at the expense of more creative curricular approaches. Moreover, should assessment be specifically tied to this core knowledge there is the danger of the 'tail wagging the dog', with the focus being put on rote learning at the expense of a cross-curricular approach. It is hard to see how the working definition proposed by Jonathan Savage in the core book of this series – that 'a cross-curricular approach to teaching is characterised by sensitivity towards, and a synthesis of, knowledge, skills and understandings from various subject areas' – could work if such a blunt assessment tool were deployed.

It has been proposed in the 2010 White Paper that more teacher training should be done 'on the job'. It could be argued that such a move will strengthen cross-curricular approaches. More time spent in schools will mean greater exposure to a range of different subjects and ways of working across subject boundaries. What can only be covered quite superficially in a university-based system can be experienced every day, with the trainees able to immerse themselves in the day-to-day planning and delivery of such approaches.

However, this highly optimistic view presupposes a number of quite important conditions. Firstly, that the schools the trainees spends time in bring them into contact with genuinely high-quality models of cross-curricular learning. The evidence of this book is that such models are hard to find at present. Indeed, we have found many schools still reluctant to explore cross-curricular working in a meaningful way. Secondly, as this book has made clear throughout, the foundation of any high-quality cross-curricular work is a good understanding of one's own subject discipline, combined with a willingness to engage in understanding the discipline of other subjects. Such development has been a strength of current teacher-training courses, and this principally comes from the university-based element. There is also an extensive body of research about effective teacher training and so there are clear lessons to be learnt here. Although it is clear that many trainees enjoy their time in school, they also quickly become socialised into school practice; this is less of a problem if that practice is of good quality, but even if it were of the highest quality trainee teachers need to have their horizons expanded. In part this can be achieved through spending time in different school settings, but university training also has a key role to play here.

Trainee teachers need a combination of challenge and support in order to develop; much of this can come from schools, but schools are often under extreme pressures to meet certain targets which can distort what happens in the classroom; for example, assessment for learning is often distorted to meet a school's need to 'measure' progress rather than support students' development. University-based training provides a space where educational practice can be examined more objectively, and different perspectives and ways of doing things can be explored, which can be later tested in school. Such work should not be underestimated.

One thing that is certain in education is that change will happen in some form. This does raise substantial challenges, not least the question of what we are training teachers to be able to do. Since Standards were introduced which trainee teachers had to meet, there have been four different versions of the Standards. It seems that what we want teachers to be able to do does change. Training courses have also had to respond to government initiatives in schools, even though many of these have proved transitory. Training courses have nonetheless focused on producing good subject teachers (it seems ironic that the government is seeking to undermine this system at a point where it is trying to promote the importance of subject teaching!). As we have argued throughout this book, good cross-curricular work has to be built on a deep understanding of subjects. Therefore to weaken this aspect of a teacher's development could fatally undermine any attempt to develop a teacher's ability to work with other subject areas.

Other questions arise that are perhaps beyond the scope of this book but will clearly have an impact in the medium to long-term development of cross-curricular approaches to the humanities. Employability remains a key concern for those involved with young people – what skills do young people need and what can humanities offer? If the emphasis within the economy remains on the STEM subjects and this continues to be reflected in higher education funding, what will this mean for humanities in schools? If there is a move towards compulsory humanities beyond KS3, what are the threats and opportunities that trend offers, and in particular how are we to cater for the full range of ability? More broadly what is a suitable humanities education for the twenty-first century? What range of humanities is necessary for a globalised society?

Practical task 8.1

As government policy develops it is inevitable that the areas discussed above will change. How does current policy at the time of reading influence your plans for cross-curricular learning?

Consider:

* ★ What can be ignored?
* ★ What cannot be ignored?
* ★ What represents an opportunity?
* ★ What represents a threat?
* ★ How will this influence your short, medium and long-term planning?

The answers to these questions are likely to need continual adjustment as policy changes. What will you do to keep abreast of these changes? The education section of the BBC website is a good starting point for this, www.bbc.co.uk/news/education.

However, are we perhaps putting too much emphasis on the impact of a changing educational landscape? Curriculum change in particular, like any form of policy implementation, tends to be a long process and outcomes are often unpredictable and unexpected. And, as Neil Thompson commented in his Key Stage History blog on 23 January 2011, 'Taking on the "specified content" battle will then be a breeze – because we all know it's daft and can subvert it anyway, as most of us have been doing since 1990!' Of course, this needs to be balanced against the fact that, as we explored in the opening chapters of this book, the confidence to subvert can only come from a deep understanding of the subject and a strong subject identity for the teacher. Those who lack specialist insights are less able to resist initiative demands, which further emphasises the need for humanities subject specialists.

Given the uncertain landscape we face, it may be more productive to shift our focus onto what we believe are the core messages that emerge from the previous chapters and reflect on what these mean for the future of cross-curricular learning in the humanities.

Reflecting on the journey so far

This book began with an exploration of the reasons why there has been a recent move towards greater cross-curricularity and the extent to which the subjects are similar by looking at the nature and purpose of each subject. In Chapter 2 we developed this into a rationale for a cross-curricular approach to different curriculum models, concluding however that the individual teacher needed to 'buy in' to this in order for it to be effective, and that in fact this individual role was the key factor in moving towards cross-curricularity. Similarly, Savage (2011) has explored this through the work of Stenhouse and his famous statement that 'there is no meaningful and long-lasting curriculum development without teacher development' (Stenhouse, 1975: 142). The remaining chapters gave an opportunity to consider approaches which can be used by any individual as a means of promoting a more effective cross-curricular approach. Thus issues relating to effective pedagogy were explored (Chapter 3), focusing on teaching concepts and content before moving on to consider more specific issues relating to enquiry and independent learning (Chapter 4), and using talk (Chapter 5). In Chapter 6 this methodology was used to explore in detail, through one aspect of the humanities, how teaching controversial and sensitive topics can be addressed through a common methodology that takes advantage of the content and concepts of the humanities subjects. Chapter 7 then explored the implications of this methodology for assessment and progression.

The remainder of this chapter will reconsider this journey in the light of the aforementioned changing political landscape, leading to a wider consideration of the possible future for cross-curricular education over the next 15 years.

The future possibilities for cross-curricular teaching and learning in the humanities

So where does this leave us if we wish to plot a future direction? If the responsibility for the development of cross-curricular approaches to the humanities in the classroom lies chiefly with the individual teacher, it is worth considering the personal journeys of the authors.

Case study 8.1: *From hedgehog to fox: one teacher's journey*

I began my journey through the labyrinthine world of curriculum design as a new head of history. In the rush of excitement engendered by a fresh revision of the National Curriculum that appeared to offer a way past the monolithic period 'blocks' of the past, I began to see new ways of designing a curriculum. Carefully chosen questions allowed pupils to make links forwards, backwards, across and within periods; models of progression underpinned a curriculum that seemed to genuinely offer an exciting and coherent way to enable pupils of all abilities to engage in the study of the past. Then came promotion and a chance to take on a whole range of subjects, and that's where the trouble started.

Power can be seductive. So can apparently elegant solutions to the conundrum of getting subjects to work together effectively in a secondary school. I began with asking 'What are we trying to achieve?', spending a lengthy period focusing on the needs of the pupils. This generated a clear underpinning set of skills and attitudes that subjects could then begin to fit around. Quickly considering the organisation of learning, I rushed to timetable models, overarching themes and some very impressive-looking diagrams. The hedgehog by now had very much emerged

---

from hibernation and was taking on the proportion of a Japanese movie monster, rolling its way across subjects in its quest for a single unifying vision that would sweep all before it.

People liked this model. By which I mean other hedgehogs. Some pupils also liked it. And some teachers. But most didn't. And it was only when the monster hedgehog finally remembered to ask the teachers their views again that sanity returned. The teachers did not want this model, but moreover many didn't need it. They may have benefited from the chance of working closely with others outside their subject area, but this led to all sorts of interesting and unpredictable directions that did not necessarily fit with the overall model. As the hedgehog began to retreat, this seemed not so much a problem as an opportunity. It was then that the fox began to emerge, sniffing curiously around these innovations, far more interested in teacher-led directions than the big, shiny model in which the hedgehog had invested so much time and personal capital.

This is not to say the hedgehog fully returned to hibernation. It still occasionally tries to emerge, straining to get out. It is constantly fed by stories of the glories of many-layered, gloriously interwoven curriculum models. But the fox has the upper hand now and that seems a much healthier state of affairs for all involved.

Case study 8.2: *Hedgehog to fox ... to magpie?*

Being appointed as a head of department after only two years experience was for me a huge challenge. I could not describe myself as a hedgehog or a fox at that point – more as a rabbit caught in headlights. Everything was so overwhelming. To make matters worse – or better, it depends which way you look at it – my department was made up of three NQTs who I had to lead to a great new future. I had barely lost my teacher L plates and here I was trying to teach three others to drive, and write schemes of work, and get my head around the thorny issue of assessment, and generally try and work out how to teach my subject well. What I inherited from my predecessor was the grand total of nothing. No schemes of work worth teaching, no assessment policy, no decent resources. At this point I suppose I was a trainee hedgehog.

Working in a relatively challenging comprehensive I soon noticed that the students struggled with literacy. Like any self-respecting trainee hedgehog I moaned about and blamed the English teachers in the school. What were they doing? Why couldn't they teach the kids to write properly? All I needed my esteemed colleagues to do was to teach the pupils how to construct a paragraph; surely any self-respecting English teacher could manage such a simple task? Throughout this period of blame, I never once thought that I needed to get out and sniff like a fox – go and steal the ideas from others and teach the kids myself how to write well. Blame is so much easier.

However, all of this changed when I ventured to a national subject-specific conference – a grand meeting of all hedgehogs as it were. But were the workshop leaders really hedgehogs? One session that I attended focused on extending writing. It really changed my views. One phrase the workshop leader used has stuck with me: 'If they ain't hearing it, you ain't saying it!' Put simply, if my kids couldn't write well in my subject it was down to me to teach them how to. Blaming the English department was a waste of my energy. A better use of energy was this: Steal ideas from English colleagues and use them for my own ends. Luckily this particular speaker was a veritable 'Artful Dodger' – he had already stolen the necessary goods and was happy to share them with us. He modelled for us how to help the students write, and demonstrated that they needed to be able to organise their ideas first, and stressed the fact that they could only write well if they were shown how to by the teacher. The penny dropped. I went back to my classroom with my new stolen tricks. And wow did they work! My kids were using connectives way before any National Strategy white folder appeared on SLT's shelves. In fact it was way before SLTs were called SLTs – they were 'senior managers' in those days! Paragraphs were modelled, essays were constructed, highlighter pens were purchased and results increased rapidly. I was hooked; my ears twitched and my nose could sniff out any decent teaching idea that might work in my classroom.

Every year I ventured off for more valuable subject-specific inset – and any useful inset I could find. I learnt from my new friends fox-like cunning. Steal, steal and steal again. I learnt that the best thing to do was talk to different colleagues in my school. I saw how to use art in my lessons. Paintings are a rich source of evidence, but what was the best way to help students read them? I picked up a handful of different strategies for this. I learnt about the power of ICT to help students think. Low-level ICT packages – word processing packages – allowed the students to do high-level thinking. I discovered the seductive tendencies of mathematics: the power of graphs to help show meaning, the beauty of statistical analysis to deepen understanding.

Throughout this period of discovery I still firmly believed I was a hedgehog. I was fully focused on one thing: creating a single box of tricks that could to help me teach my subject better. I didn't realise that all of this stolen booty might actually mean that I was a fox – or was I? I still don't know. All I know is that talking to other teachers in other departments and asking them how they manage to do certain things – with data or paintings or poems – really can have a massive impact in your own classroom. Students do not transfer what they do from one lesson to another naturally, especially if teachers are essentially teaching the same concept but doing it in slightly different ways. Knowledge is power here. Knowing how the English teachers help students construct paragraphs and using the same techniques as they do helps the students transfer their understanding across the subjects. Simple phrases like, 'in English you do this; well it is exactly the same in this subject,' are exceedingly helpful. Talking to other subject specialists and finding out how they approach certain things widens one's own understanding and can help students make the connections we want them to. Teachers talking about teaching is a powerful tool – but few school leaders value it enough to allow it to happen regularly. Taking a theme that allows us to teach a number of different subjects historically and geographically and artistically and musically *and* shows the students connections is a great idea. But this comes with a health warning: forcing links where they are tenuous or where they simply don't exist is a futile exercise.

Also, my experience as a humanities adviser, reviewing a number of competency-style curricula, has left me in little doubt that such integrated schemes are not the magic bullet they have been sold as. They are not a bad idea necessarily. But the learning that I have seen take place in nearly all these classrooms has been no better than the learning that takes place in a normal history, or geography, or RE classroom. Some teachers who teach such courses are not subject experts and are confused by the 'skills vs knowledge' argument. Many think that it is fine to teach students certain 'soft skills' such as how to work well in groups and manage time more effectively – all useful, but if the children are not learning anything else then this worries me. I believe that these skills/PLTS/competences should be a complement to, and not a replacement of, the conceptual building blocks that underpin history and geography as disciplines. Children go to school to learn about things that they cannot learn at home or at a sports club. The 'soft skills' can be taught in a humanities classroom *and* children learn the great things the humanities subjects can teach, including the intrinsically interesting stories, the important substantive knowledge and, to a greater or lesser degree, depending on the humanities subject, the disciplined thinking that the subjects teach. Non-specialists often do not have the expertise to do all of this.

So have I become a hedgehog or a fox? I'm still not sure. But I do know that when it comes to great teaching ideas, I am definitely a magpie.

Case study 8.3: *From hedgehog to fox (or perhaps not quite!)*

My development as teacher, and more latterly as someone who trains teachers, often raises more questions than it resolves, or at the very least identifies tensions between what I believe and do. Cross-curricular working is one such example.

As a subject specialist I am steeped in my subject's traditions and fundamentally believe that as a subject it has immense educative power, which I do not wish to see diminished. On the other hand I can appreciate the value and benefits of cross-curricular approaches to teaching.

As a teacher I have had to teach across the humanities subjects (although these were often taught separately as subjects), yet I could always see the benefits of geography in understanding history (having read the classic book *The Making of the English Landscape* by W.G. Hoskins, I would love to be able to 'read' the landscape and use that to enhance my understanding of the past!). I feel that citizenship is a lesser subject without a historical input, and the issues often raised in RE are timeless questions about humanity which you can see recurring throughout the past. There is much to be gained by students from bringing together the combined insights into human action and nature which the humanities subjects provide. Yet, and it is a very big and important yet, the power of those subjects will be diminished if they are brought together in artificial ways, or where the concepts and processes that underpin the subjects are neglected. Too often the work I have seen in practice does a disservice to the subjects. This is quite often for apparently very legitimate reasons such as trying to develop students' teamworking skills, but this neglects two important issues: firstly, such skills can be developed through rigorous teaching of subjects, and secondly, at secondary school we often forget that KS3 is the only place in the curriculum where students will receive subject-specialist teaching in many of the humanities subjects. Thus to deny students access to the distinctive nature of these subjects is a matter of serious concern.

In many ways I feel like an unreformed hedgehog, wedded to the idea of a curriculum where separate, discrete subjects are identifiable, yet as a curious fox I can see the power of drawing on the combined insights of the different subjects. For me, however, many of the issues that have emerged in the writing of this book are less to do with the curriculum and what pupils study (although clearly this is important), and more to do with how students are taught. Students need those 'transferable skills' and need to encounter them in all their subject areas so that they become adept at problem solving, working effectively in groups and so forth, but they also need to be helped to see how the subjects they study are valuable, how they actually offer different insights into issues studied and the world in which we live.

There is no magic answer to the conundrum of cross-curricular teaching and learning; instead there are lots of questions. I know many people look for models that 'work', arguing that we do not need to reinvent the wheel, but actually I think we need to keep reinventing wheels – a tractor's wheel doesn't fit on a Mini and vice versa, so we actually have to fit wheels to specific circumstances. This puts much of the responsibility onto individual teachers and, busy as we are, I think that this is empowering for teachers and is part and parcel of a teacher's sense of identity and personal development. So read the book, reflect seriously on the issues it raises, but ultimately it is up to you to make of it what you will!

> ## Reflective task 8.2
>
> These are the personal journeys of three different people in different positions. Yet there may be common threads that run through their experiences. What are these?
>
> Where would you personally position yourself within the hedgehog/fox metaphor? Has this changed during the course of your teaching experience? How might it change further in the future in the light of changes to the educational landscape? Are there aspects of your beliefs and values that have been challenged, developed or consolidated by your reading of this book?

Perhaps the lesson of these case studies is that there is no lesson. Teachers have to find their own way if they are to successfully address cross-curricular teaching and learning. None of these authors arrived at the point of wanting to write this book without taking many twists and turns in their thinking and classroom practice. Thus it seems the point is less the end result than the journey itself. It is these individual journeys, or rather the way individual teachers reflect on these journeys and use them to develop their own cross-curricular methodology, that will count.

The case studies do however reflect two common themes which have repeatedly appeared in this book. Firstly the power of collaboration; each of us has at some stage been challenged, inspired and surprised by the experience of working with colleagues from other subject disciplines, both within and beyond the humanities. It is this opportunity to move outside the boundaries of the subject that has often provided the most thought-provoking career moments and led to an enriched pedagogy. Yet the second theme has always tempered this, the absolute conviction that subjects really matter and that any move to work across disciplines is always rooted in a desire to develop one's own subject. The commitment this lends to the individual teacher is a huge factor in the development of cross-curricular approaches.

The future will depend on how teachers choose to respond to the challenges of books like this and their wider reflection on their own practice. External influences will always matter, but it is clear that top-down initiatives simply don't work. Where they are effective it is because subject teachers make them work, and rarely in the way that was intended by those who designed them. Therefore the future lies squarely in the hands of the humanities teacher to build the future, cross-curricular or otherwise.

For this teacher-led approach to work in anything other than a piecemeal way, it will be essential to find platforms through which teachers can share their stories. This does not mean the uncritical sharing of 'good practice' that is too often seen in both centrally produced reports and schools' own self-evaluation materials. Rather it is ensuring teachers have the chance to evaluate their own cross-curricular methodology and share it with others, empowering teachers to do this in a way that is systematic and easy to access. Where can the geography teacher go today to genuinely engage with such a process? If a history teacher experiences real success with a cross-curricular approach, how can this be then be shared beyond the confines of their own school? How would an RE teacher be able to build on this success in a different context?

It will also be essential that the humanities subjects continue to assert their identities through such debate and research. Competing ideologies will continue to predict the demise or renaissance of 'subjects'. If our subjects matter to us – and they surely must – then we must be prepared to re-think our subjects in the light of changing pedagogical frameworks, new ideas about learning, and the changing curriculum designs that usually follow in their wake. We must be confident enough to assert that our subjects do matter and are relevant, but also maintain 'sensitivity towards, and a synthesis of, knowledge, skills and understanding from various subject areas' (Savage, 2011).

As new teachers enter the profession they will change things in ways we cannot yet perceive. Perhaps they will be naturally inclined to think in a cross-curricular way, having been increasingly educated in such a way. Or maybe they will react against negative experiences of such courses and be better disposed to a subject-specific approach. But we hope that whatever the future may hold, this book might lay the foundations for a review of the way we currently see cross-curricular learning in the humanities and a response to the challenges of the future.

Professional standards for QTS

This chapter will help you meet the following Q standards: Q6, Q7a, Q8, Q10, Q11, Q14.

Professional standards for teachers

This chapter will help you meet the following core standards: C6, C7, C8, C15, C16, C30, C40, C41.

References

Banks, J.A. (2006) 'Varieties of history: Negro, black, white', in J.A. Banks, *Race, Culture and Education: The selected works of James A. Banks.* London, Routledge.

Barton, K. and Levstik, L. (2004) *Teaching History for the Common Good.* Mahwah, NJ, Lawrence Erlbaum Associates.

Bates, N., Herrity, S. and McFahn, R. (2009) 'Riots, railways and a Hampshire hill fort: exploiting local history for rigorous evidential enquiry'. *Teaching History* 134, 16–23.

Berlin, I. (1953) *The Hedgehog and the Fox: An essay on Tolstoy's view of history.* London, Weidenfeld & Nicolson.

Black, P. and Wiliam, D. (1998) *Inside the Black Box: Raising standards through classroom assessment.* King's College London School of Education. Available from http://weaeducation.typepad.co.uk/files/blackbox-1.pdf (last accessed 14 April 2011).

Burn, K. and Harris, R. (2009) 'Findings from the Historical Association survey of secondary history teachers'. Available from http://www.history.org.uk/news/news_415.html (Last accessed on 21 February 2011).

Burnham, S. (2007) 'Getting Year 7 to set down their own questions about the Islamic Empire, 600–1600'. *Teaching History* 128, 11–16.

Burnham, S. and Brown, G. (2004) 'Assessment without level descriptions'. *Teaching History* 115, 5–15.

Byrom, J. (2003) 'Continuity and progression', in M. Riley and R. Harris (eds), *Past Forward: A vision for school history, 2002–2012.* London, Historical Association.

Cotton, D. (2006) 'Teaching controversial environmental issues: neutrality and balance in the reality of the classroom'. *Educational Research* 48: 2, 223–41.

Counsell, C. (1999) 'Editorial'. *Teaching History* 98, 2.

DCSF/QCA (2007) *The National Curriculum Statutory Requirements for Key Stages 3 and 4.* London, QCA.

DfE (1995) *History in the National Curriculum.* London, DfE.

DfE (2010) 'The Importance of Teaching: the Schools White Paper 2010'. Available from http://www.education.gov.uk/publications/standard/publicationdetail/page1/CM%20 7980 (last accessed 9 April 2011).

DfEE/QCA (1999) *The National Curriculum for England: Handbook for secondary school teachers in England. Key Stages 3 and 4.* London, DfEE/QCA.

DfES (2007) *Diversity and Citizenship Curriculum Review.* London, DfES.

Edwards, D. and Mercer, N. (1987) *Common Knowledge: The development of understanding in the classroom.* London, Methuen.

Erricker, C. (2010) *Religious Education: A conceptual and interdisciplinary approach for secondary level*. London, Routledge.

Farmer, A. and Knight, P. (1995) *Active History in Key Stages 3 and 4*. London, David Fulton.

Faulks, K. (2006) 'Education for citizenship in English secondary schools: a critique of current principle and practice'. *Journal of Education Policy* 21: 1, 59–74.

Fenwick, T. (2003) 'The "good" teacher in a neo-liberal risk society: a Foucaultian analysis of professional growth plans'. *Journal of Curriculum Studies* 35: 3, 335–54.

Gardner, H. (2007) *Five Minds for the Future*. Boston, MA, Harvard Business School Press.

Gipps, C. and Stobbart, G. (1993) *Assessment: A teacher's guide to the issues*. London, Hodder and Stoughton.

Gorman, M. (1998) 'The "structured enquiry" is not a contradiction in terms'. *Teaching History* 92, 20–5.

Gove, M. (2010) 'Speech to the Conservative Party Conference, 5 October 2010'. Available from http://www.conservatives.com/News/Speeches/2010/10/Michael_Gove_All_pupils_will_learn_our_island_story.aspx (last accessed 11 March 2011).

Grimmit, M. (2000) *Pedagogies of Religious Education*. Great Waking, Essex, McCrimmons.

Haenen, J. and Tuithof, H. (2008) 'Cooperative learning: the place of pupil involvement in a history textbook'. *Teaching History* 131, 30–4.

Halton, M.J. (2004) 'Putting professional development into action by putting action into professional development in second level schools in Ireland'. *Educational Action Research* 12: 1, 127–44.

Hann, T. (2010) 'Are you outstanding? Are they outstanding because of you?'. Available from http://www.northallertoncoll.org.uk/CPD/Articles/Are-you-outstandind.pdf (last accessed 14 April 2011).

Harris, R. (2010) *An Action Research Project to Promote the Teaching of Culturally and Ethnically Diverse History on a Secondary Postgraduate Certificate of Education History Course*. Unpublished PhD, University of Southampton.

Harris, R. and Haydn, T. (2006) 'Pupils' enjoyment of history: what lessons can teachers learn from their pupils?'. *Curriculum Journal* 17: 4, 315–33.

Harris, R. and Luff, I. (2004) *Meeting SEN in History*. London, David Fulton.

Harris, R. and Ratcliffe, M. (2005) 'Socio-scientific issues and the quality of exploratory talk: what can be learned from schools involved in a 'collapsed day' project?'. *Curriculum Journal* 16: 4, 439–53.

Haydn, T., Arthur, J. and Hunt, M. (1997) *Learning to Teach History in the Secondary School*. London, Routledge.

Heater, D. (1999) *What is Citizenship?* London, Polity Press.

Historical Association (2007) *Teaching Emotive and Controversial History*. Available from http://www.history.org.uk/resources/secondary_resource_780.html (last accessed 9 April 2011).

Hopkin, J. (2006) 'Level descriptions and assessment: a discussion paper for the GA'. Available from http://www.geography.org.uk/download/GA_AULevelAssessmentsInGeography.pdf (last accessed 9 April 2011).

Hopwood, N. (2007) 'GTIP think piece: values and controversial Issues'. Available from http://www.geography.org.uk/gtip/thinkpieces/valuesandcontroversialissues/ (last accessed 26 November 2010).

Hoskins, W.G. (1955) *The Making of the English Landscape*. Leicester, Penguin History.

Husbands, C. (1996) *What is History Teaching?* Buckingham, Open University Press.

Illingworth, S. (2000) 'Hearts, minds and souls: exploring values through history'. *Teaching History* 100, 20–4.

Joyce, B., Calhoun, E. and Hopkins, D. (1997) *Models for Learning – Tools for Teaching*. Buckingham, Open University Press.

Kagan, S. (1994) *Cooperative Learning*. San Clemente, CA, Kagan Publishing.

Keast, J. (2003) 'Citizenship in the National Curriculum', in L. Gearon (ed.), *Learning to teach Citizenship in the Secondary School*. London, RoutledgeFalmer.

Kent, A. (2002) 'Geography: changes and challenges', in M. Smith (ed.), *Teaching Geography in Secondary Schools: A reader*. London, RoutledgeFalmer/Open University Press.

Kinloch, N. (2001) 'Parallel catastrophes? Uniqueness, redemption and the Shoah'. *Teaching History* 104, 8–14.

Kitson, A. (2007a) 'Teaching history in Northern Ireland: creating an oasis of calm?', in A. McCully (ed.), *Recent Research on Teaching History in Northern Ireland: Informing curriculum change*. Ulster, University Of Ulster/UNESCO Centre.

Kitson, A. (2007b) 'History teaching and reconciliation in Northern Ireland', in E. Cole (ed.), *Teaching the Violent Past: History education and reconciliation*. Boulder, CO, Rowman and Littlefield.

Kitson, A. and McCully, A. (2005) '"You hear about it for real in school." Avoiding, containing and risk-taking in the classroom'. *Teaching History* 120, 32–7.

Kiwan, D. (2008) 'Citizenship education in England at the cross-roads? Four models of citizenship and their implications for ethnic and religious diversity'. *Oxford Review of Education* 34: 1, 39–58.

Klaassen, C.A. (2002) 'Teacher pedagogical competence and sensibility'. *Teaching and Teacher Education* 18, 151–8.

Kohlberg, L. (1981) *Essays on Moral Development, Vol. I: The philosophy of moral development*. San Francisco, CA, Harper & Row.

Kutnick, P., Sebba, J., Blatchford, P., Galton, M. and Thorp, J. (2005) *The Effects of Pupil Grouping: Literature review. Research Report 688*. Nottingham, DfES Publications.

Lambert, D. (2004) 'Geography in the Holocaust: citizenship denied'. *Teaching History* 116, 42–8.

Lambert, D. (2010) 'Issues in Geography Education: Session 8. Progression'. Available from http://www.geography.org.uk/download/GA_PRMGHProgressionThinkPiece.pdf (last accessed 9 April 2011).

Lambert, D. and Balderstone, D. (2010) *Learning to Teach Geography in the Secondary School* (2nd edn). London, RoutledgeFalmer.

Lambert, D. and Morgan, J. (2010) *Teaching Geography 11–18: A conceptual approach*. Maidenhead, Open University Press.

Lee, P. and Shemilt, D. (2003) 'A scaffold, not a cage: progression and progression models in history'. *Teaching History* 113, 13–23.

Lomas, T. (1990) *Teaching and Assessing Historical Understanding*. London, Historical Association.

McCully, A. and Pilgrim, N. (2004) 'They took Ireland away from us and we've got to fight to get it back. Using fictional characters to explore the relationship between historical interpretation and contemporary attitudes'. *Teaching History* 114, 17–21.

McFahn, R. (2011) *Teaching Historical Interpretations*. Available from http://www.historyresourcecupboard.co.uk/advice1.html (last accessed 4 March 2011).

Mercer, N. (1995) *The Guided Construction of Knowledge: Talk amongst teachers and learners*. Clevedon, Multilingual Matters.

Mercer, N. (2000) *Words and Minds: How we use language to think together*. London, Routledge.

Moss, D. (n.d.) 'Teaching the Holocaust in geography' *GeogEd* 3: 2, Article 1. Available from http://www.geography.org.uk/gtip/geogede-journal/vol3issue2/article1 (last accessed 9 April 2011).

Muijs, D. and Reynolds, D. (2005) *Effective Teaching: Evidence and practice* (2nd edn). London, Sage.

Nelson, J. (2008) 'Exploring diversity through ethos in initial teacher education'. *Teaching and Teacher Education* 24, 1729–38.

Norman, D.A. (1978) 'Notes towards a complex theory of learning', in A.M. Lesgold (ed.), *Cognitive Psychology and Instruction*. New York: Plenum.

Ofsted (2003) *Good Assessment Practice in History*. London, Ofsted.

Ofsted (2006) *Towards Consensus? Citizenship in secondary schools*. Available from http://www. ofsted.gov.uk/Ofsted-home/Publications-and-research/Browse-all-by/Education/ Curriculum/Citizenship/Secondary/Towards-consensus-Citizenship-in-secondary- schools (last accessed 9 April 2011).

Ofsted (2007) 'Making sense of religion'. Available from http://www.ofsted.gov.uk/Ofsted- home/Publications-and-research/Browse-all-by/Education/Curriculum/Religious- education/Secondary/Making-sense-of-religion (last accessed 23 February 2010).

Ofsted (2008) 'Curriculum innovation in schools'. Available from http://www.ofsted.gov.uk/ Ofsted-home/Publications-and-research/Browse-all-by/Documents-by-type/Thematic- reports/Curriculum-Innovation-in-schools (last accessed 23 February 2010).

Ofsted (2009a) 'Planning for change: the impact of the new KS3 curriculum'. Available from http://www.ofsted.gov.uk/Ofsted-home/Publications-and-research/Browse-all-by/ Documents-by-type/Thematic-reports/Planning-for-change-the-impact-of-the-new- Key-Stage-3-curriculum (last accessed 9 April 2011).

Ofsted (2009b) 'The evaluation schedule for schools: guidance and grade descriptors for inspecting schools in England under section 5 of the Education Act 2005'. Available from http://www.ofsted.gov.uk/Ofsted-home/Forms-and-guidance/Browse-all-by/Other/ General/Evaluation-schedule-of-judgements-for-schools-inspected-under-section-five- of-the-Education-Act-2005-from-September-2009 (last accessed 25 April 2011).

Ofsted (2010a) 'Citizenship established? Citizenship in schools 2006/9'. Available from http://www.ofsted.gov.uk/Ofsted-home/Publications-and-research/Browse-all-by/ Documents-by-type/Thematic-reports/Citizenship-established-Citizenship-in- schools-2006-09 (last accessed 9 April 2011).

Ofsted (2010b) 'Transforming religious education: religious education in schools 2006-09'. Available from http://www.ofsted.gov.uk/Ofsted-home/Publications-and-research/Browse- all-by/Documents-by-type/Thematic-reports/Transforming-religious-education (last accessed 25 April 2011).

Ofsted (2011a) 'Geography: learning to make a world of difference'. Available from http:// www.ofsted.gov.uk/Ofsted-home/Publications-and-research/Browse-all-by/Documents- by-type/Thematic-reports/Geography-Learning-to-make-a-world-of-difference (last accessed 9 April 2011).

Ofsted (2011b) 'History for all: history in English schools. 2007/10'. Available from http:// www.ofsted.gov.uk/Ofsted-home/Publications-and-research/Browse-all-by/Documents- by-type/Thematic-reports/History-for-all (last accessed 25 April 2011).

Oxfam (2006) 'Teaching controversial issues'. Available from http://www.oxfam.org.uk/ education/teachersupport/cpd/controversial/ (last accessed 29 November 2010).

Phillips, R. (2002) *Reflective Teaching of History 11–18*. London, Continuum.

Price, M. (1968) 'History in danger'. *History* 53, 342–7.

Pring, R. (2006) 'Against citizenship'. *Prospero* 12: 3, 54–58.

QCA (1998) *Education for Citizenship and the Teaching of Democracy in Schools*. London, QCA.

QCA (2001) *Citizenship: A scheme of work for KS3. Teacher's guide*. London, QCA.

QCA (2007) 'A framework of personal, learning and thinking skills'. Available from http:// curriculum.qcda.gov.uk/uploads/PLTS_framework_tcm8-1811.pdf (last accessed 21 June 2011).

QCA (2008a) 'A big picture of the curriculum'. Available from http://webarchive. nationalarchives.gov.uk/20081118111939/http://qca.org.uk/libraryAssets/media/Big_ Picture_2008.pdf (last accessed 9 April 2011).

QCA (2008b) *National Curriculum: Level descriptions for history*. Available from http://curriculum. qcda.gov.uk/key-stages-3-and-4/subjects/key-stage-3/history/Level-descriptions/index. aspx (last accessed 14 April 2011).

QCA (2008c) 'The diploma: an overview of the qualification'. Available from http://www.derbyshire.gov.uk/images/An%20overview%20of%20the%20qualification%20(PDF%20%20217kb)_tcm9–95782.pdf (last accessed 9 April 2011).

QCA/DfES (2004) 'Religious education: the non-statutory national framework'. Available from http://curriculum.qcda.gov.uk/uploads/Religious%20education%201999%20programme%20of%20study_tcm8–12168.pdf (last accessed 9 April 2011).

Riley, M. (2000) 'Into the KS3 history garden: choosing and planting your enquiry questions'. *Teaching History* 99, 8–13.

Roberts, M. (2003) *Learning through Enquiry: Making sense of geography in the KS3 classroom.* Sheffield, Geographical Association.

RSA (2008) 'Opening Minds impact update'. Available from http://www.thersa.org/__data/assets/pdf_file/0019/155125/RSA-Opening-minds-impact-update-2008–final.pdf (last accessed 1 January 2010).

RSA (2011) *RSA Opening Minds Competence Framework.* Available from http://www.rsaopeningminds.org.uk/ (last accessed 4 March 2011).

Rudge, L. (2000) 'The place of religious education in the curriculum', in A. Wright and A. Brandom (eds), *Learning to teach Religious Education in the Secondary School.* London, RoutledgeFalmer.

Rüsen, J. (2004) 'Historical consciousness: narrative structure, moral function, and ontological development', in P. Seixas (ed.), *Theorizing Historical Consciousness.* Toronto, University of Toronto Press.

Savage, J. (2011) *Cross-Curricular Teaching and Learning in the Secondary School.* London, Routledge.

Saxton, J. and Morgan, N. (1994) *Asking Better Questions.* London, Drake.

Scott-Baumann, A., Bloomfield, A. and Roughton, L. (1997) *Becoming a Secondary School Teacher.* London, Hodder and Stoughton.

Short, G. and Reed, C. (2004) *Issues in Holocaust Education.* Aldershot, Ashgate.

Stenhouse, L. (1975) *An Introduction to Curriculum Research and Development.* London, Heinemann.

Stephen, A. (2005) '"Why can't they just live together happily, Miss?" Unravelling the complexities of the Arab–Israeli conflict at GCSE'. *Teaching History* 120, 5–10.

Sylvester, D. (1994) 'Change and continuity in history teaching, 1900–93', in H. Bourdillon (ed.), *Teaching History.* London, Routledge/Open University Press.

Taylor, L. (2008) 'Key concepts and medium term planning'. *Teaching Geography,* 33: 2, 50–4.

Telfer, S. (2004) *What Might Progression Look Like in Geography Teaching?* (unpublished course notes). West Sussex Heads of Geography Conference (June 2000).

Thompson, N. (2009) 'KS3 teacher assessment: the 10 key principles'. Available from http://www.keystagehistory.co.uk/assessment/keystage3/A3–1.html (last accessed 14 April 2011).

Thompson, N. (2010) 'What to look for in excellent lessons: your starter for 12'. Available from http://www.keystageHistory.co.uk/teaching-approaches/keystage3/T3–2.html (last accessed 15 April 2011).

Thompson, N. (2011) 'Elusive outstanding teaching grade even harder to achieve?'. Available from http://www.blogs.keystagehistory.co.uk (last accessed 12 February 2011).

Tosh, J. (2008) *Why History Matters.* Basingstoke, Palgrave Macmillan.

Traille, E.K.A. (2006) *School History and Perspectives on the Past: A study of students of African Caribbean descent and their mothers.* Unpublished PhD, Institute of Education, University of London.

Trowler, P. (2003) *Education Policy.* Abingdon, Routledge.

Tyler, R. (1949) *Basic Principles of Curriculum and Instruction.* Chicago, University of Chicago Press.

Van Eekelen, I.M., Vermunt, J.D. and Boshuizen, H.P.A. (2006) 'Exploring teachers' will to learn'. *Teaching and Teacher Education* 22, 408–23.

Vermeulen, E. (2000) 'What is progress in history?'. *Teaching History* 98, 35–41.

Weedon, P. and Butt, G. (2009) *Assessing Progress in your KS3 Geography Curriculum*. Sheffield, Geography Association.

Weedon, P. and Butt, G. (2010), *Thinking about Progression in Geography*. Available from http://www.geography.org.uk/projects/makinggeographyhappen/progression (last accessed 14 April 2011).

Wellington, J. (1988) *Controversial Issues in the Curriculum*. Oxford, Basil Blackwell.

Wilkinson, A. (2010) 'Making cross-curricular links in history: some ways forward'. *Teaching History* 138, 4–7.

Williams, M. and Bolem, R. (1993) *The Continuing Professional Development of Teachers*. Department of Education, University College of Swansea, General Teaching Council Initiative for England and Wales.

Wood, D. (1988) *How Children Think and Learn* (2nd edn). Oxford, Blackwell.

Woodcock, J. (2010) 'Disciplining cross-curricularity'. *Teaching History* 138, 8–12.

Wragg, E.C. and Brown, G. (2001) *Questioning in the Secondary School*. London, RoutledgeFalmer.

Wrenn, A. (2010) 'History's secret weapon: the enquiry of a disciplined mind'. *Teaching History* 138, 32–40.

Young, M. (2008) *Bringing Knowledge Back In: From social constructivism to social realism in the sociology of education*. Abingdon, Routledge.

Index

Printed in Great Britain
by Amazon